The Sporting Chef's Favorite

WILD GAME RECIPES

By
Scott Leysath

Arrowhead Classics, Inc.

New York - Sacramento - Sevierville, Tennessee

Copyright © 1997 by Arrowhead Classics, Inc. All rights reserved.

No part of this publication may be reproduced in any manner whatsoever without permission in writing from the publisher except in the case of brief quotations embodied in reviews or articles. Making copies of this book is a violation of U.S. copyright laws. For information address Arrowhead Classics, Inc. at arrohead@arrowhead-classics.com or visit our web page at: www.arrowhead-classics.com, to learn more about us.

All recipes	Scott Leysath
Edited	Judie Wilson
	Claudia Newcorn
	Maureen McCarthy
Color Photography	Donald A. Gazzaniga
B&W photography	Stephanie Wilson
Cover design and Graphics	The Graphics Company, Loomis, CA 95650
Page Layout and Typography	WK Graphics & Design, 4263 Niblick Way, Fair Oaks, CA 95628
	Circle D Graphics, Los Angeles, CA 91601

Wild Game Paintings provided by artist, Joe Garcia. Color prints of each painting are available through Spinetta Winery And Gallery, 12557 Steiner Road, Plymouth, CA 95669. 209-245-3384.

Campfire Ink Drawing (Page 59) by Larry Nielson
Larry Nielson, P. O. Box 2329, No. Hollywood, CA 91610-0329

This edition published by Arrowhead Classics, Inc.
P. O. Box 4189
Sevierville, TN 37864

ISBN 1-886571-02-3
Library of Congress Catalog Card Number: 96-083897

Second Printing. Printed in Hong Kong.
9 8 7 6 5 4 3

SCOTT LEYSATH

Scott Leysath has been an avid hunter, fisherman and outdoorsman since he was a young boy. Even back then Scott insisted on cooking his own game, much to the dismay of his mother and father. Lucky us! During those years Scott learned the basics of good camp cooking, while foregoing the usual freeze-dried foods and canned stews.

After earning his college degree at the University of Arizona, Scott decided to turn his cooking skills into his profession. He accepted a position with Grand American Fare, a 33 unit restaurant chain where he perfected his many recipes for nine years. He was Vice President of GAF when he left in 1986 to become a partner in a famous Sacramento, California restaurant — *Peter B's Freeport Inn*. As co-owner of Peter B's, Scott featured game dishes nightly. Peter B's soon became famous for its wild game meals.

Scott has appeared as a guest chef on west coast CBS and NBC affiliate TV stations. His game cooking prowess has also been featured in several metropolitan area newspapers and magazines. He is actively involved with numerous sportsman's groups including California Waterfowl Association, Ducks Unlimited, The National Wild Turkey Federation and the Safari Club International.

During the past five years, Scott has conducted wild game cooking demonstrations for national department store chains, as well as outdoor groups like the California Waterfowl Association Annual Convention, and Ducks Unlimited. Each year the popularity of the seminars has grown dramatically. Realizing the demand for game preparation instruction, Scott, in association with Hollywood entertainer Wil Shriner, has produced a video tape, *The Sporting Chef's Famous Wild Game Recipes*. The video is available in most stores or through *Arrowhead Classcis at 1-800 886 4538 or on the web at www.arrowhead-classics.com.*

Cover photo: Scott Leysath cooks his favorite grouse recipe at Sardine Lake below the California Sierra Buttes mountain range north of Downieville and Sierra City.

Back cover: Sardine Lake.

You can order a copy of this book and the Chef's video by calling 1-800-886 4538 or you may access the World Wide Web for more information about Arrowhead Classics books at,

www.arrowhead-classics.com

Contents

Wild Game Cooking

Few experiences compare to the exhilaration of a successful hunting or fishing adventure. After much planning and anticipation, we who hunt set out in search of a limit of big game, trophy sized fish or game birds. It's amazing how we are able to wake up before our alarm clocks sound when the day's activity promises an outdoor adventure rather than a day at the office.

While the taking of game during the outdoor experience is what motivates most of us to brave otherwise intolerable weather, marshes, high mountains and a long hike through pant-ripping briar thickets, too few of us enjoy the cooking and eating of game. Too often you may hear expressions of dislike for wild game dishes. There's a reason. Many people have had an unpleasant experience with improperly prepared or handled game. They have been operating under the misconception that game is tough, when in reality it is often the lack of good care, and sometimes poor preparation that has made it so. Another reason could be that recipes handed down from generation to generation may not satisfy today's more sophisticated palates. The recipes in this book, are contemporary and money saving in that you use little fuel energy and fewer fats, and develop a lot more flavor and enjoyment. Those who have not tried wild game for years are usually surprised to discover how incredibly delicious properly prepared game dishes taste. I know. I have been cooking game for public palates for years, and I've fed many converts.

Still, on numerous occasions, I have had disheartening discussions with hunters regarding the preparation of wild game. One gentleman explained how he removes the unpleasant taste from pheasant by soaking the bird in buttermilk for twenty-four hours before deep-fat frying it. After that, he smothers it with brown gravy. Unbelievably to me, the birds he spoke of had been plump farm-raised versions that could hardly have tasted much different than chicken. I believe that given the choice between the aforementioned dish and a pheasant deftly prepared, the diner will choose the latter. Try one of my recipes for pheasant in this book. You'll find yourself returning to this book more and more.

Introducing Wild Game Meals to Friends

Introducing newcomers to wild game meals requires some careful planning. For instance, you can't plop a whole roasted duck down in front of a guest and expect anything less than apprehension from them. Remember, we eat with our eyes as well as our mouths. To help make the visual part of the meal more appetizing, try removing the breast from the carcass and letting it stand for a moment to allow the juices to drain. Then, slice the meat at an angle and fan out the slices from a focal point as you would a work of art. Finish the dish with a rich and flavorful sauce and serve with a complementary side dish or two. Along with presenting game in an attractive manner, two main principals of game cooking will guarantee great meals: All game must be handled properly and please, don't over cook your game.

1. All Game Must Be Handled Properly.

When you purchase meat, poultry or fish at a market, it usually comes neatly packaged and labeled. For instance, if you notice that one package of beef looks a little discolored from the others, you will probably opt for the "healthier" appearing one. The discoloration of the package you reject results from exposure to oxygen. The same thing happens to your game when it has been exposed to heat or air, or when it has not been properly cleaned, dressed and stored.

Care of Hunted Meat

At the hunt, or immediately upon taking large game, it is important to clean and cool it as soon as possible. Rinse with cold water and either get it to the butcher, (my usual recommendation), or butcher it yourself. I do not recommend hanging or aging game for extended periods of more than a week or two, unless you have access to a temperature-controlled aging locker. Your best bet is to cool it and wrap it carefully before clearly labeling each package with a permanent marker. Include the type of animal (deer, elk, moose), the cut of meat (chop, roast, stew) and the date of packaging.

Storing Wild Game

Plan ahead before storing game birds and small game. In many instances, you can make more judicious use of freezer space by removing the meat from the animals and wrapping the disjointed carcasses separately for use in game stocks. Once I have enough carcasses to make a hearty stock, I remove them from the freezer and undertake the task of preparing a variety of stocks that are then frozen in small quantities in concentrated form for use throughout the year.

Regardless of how you wrap your game before freezing, do so carefully. Exposure to oxygen is the worst enemy of all meats. Make certain that all packages are wrapped tightly.

One of the greatest inventions designed to help us with preserving food that we want to save for future cooking, is the home vacuum packaging system. Vacuum packaging insures that stored game is not exposed to oxygen when used with the proper storage bags. This eliminates spoilage and freezer burn, which occurs no matter how well a prod-

uct is wrapped. Vacuum packaged fish and game are more easily stored; the packages take up less freezer space and they can be thawed by simply placing the sealed packages in cold water. I vacuum package even those items I do not intend to freeze, but need to keep fresh for up to a week. I prefer the FoodSaver™ unit for its ease of operation, affordability and durability. FoodSaver™ patented VacLoc® bags don't leak, and the contents remain significantly fresher than those stored in plastic containers or zipper-lock type bags, usually extending shelf life 3 to 5 times longer than traditional storage methods. The modest cost of one of these handy units is outweighed by its utility. Freezing small game, waterfowl and game birds in milk cartons filled with water also works well. I have found that they can be frozen for a year or so with good results. The biggest drawback of this method is the amount of space necessary to store frozen milk cartons. Thawing is also cumbersome.

I rarely freeze big game backstraps or tenderloins. Assuming they make it to my kitchen, I refrigerate them for only a day or two before cooking. The same goes with large drake mallards or other large ducks. They do seem to taste better within the week they were shot.

Although certain precautions will guarantee that your game has the best chance of retaining the most flavor during prolonged freezing, properly handled fresh game will almost always taste better than frozen game. The only exception would be an animal that has been feeding on unsavory items that may affect the flavor of the meat. Sometimes we can do all the right things in terms of preparation, yet unpleasant flavors prevail. Such is the chance one takes when cooking wild game.

Fat and sinew should be trimmed from all large game animals. Most unpleasant flavors can be attributed to the fat of the animals. Replace the natural fat from game animals with commercial substitutes, such as bacon or butter.

2. Do Not Overcook Your Game

If you want the very best flavor and tenderness from your wild game, do not cook it past medium-rare. Beyond medium-rare, game will toughen up and develop the dreaded "gamy" flavor and texture. Game meats are extremely lean, making them unforgiving when they are overcooked. Meat can turn from being perfect to having the texture of shoe leather in a matter of minutes. Therefore, it is recommended that you remove the meat from the heat source just before it reaches the desired temperature. If you should miss the mark, the only way to rescue overcooked game is to cook it for an hour or two in liquid until the meat becomes tender and starts to fall apart. The finished product will certainly be edible, but the flavor and texture will be more reminiscent of stewed meat than the delicious flavors you would have had otherwise.

A good meat thermometer will help you get a feel for when to remove game from the flame. Game birds should not be cooked past 150°F degrees. Antlered game is medium-rare at 135°F. Ducks and geese should be removed at 140°F and 130°F, respectively. Because of possible risk of exposure to trichinosis, bear and wild boar should be cooked to a safe internal temperature of 140°F. After using the meat thermometer a time or two, learn to trust your judgment when cooking wild game. As the meat cooks, apply pressure to the flesh with your fingers. The meat will yield to pressure less and less as it cooks. When in doubt, pull it out of the oven or skillet and test for doneness. Most meats, especially large cuts, will continue to cook a bit after they have been removed from the heat. It is far better to remove game that has been slightly undercooked than to overcook it.

When The Fat Is Gone

The nutritional benefits of wild and farm-raised game are superior to commercially-raised beef, pork and poultry. Game is usually seven to ten times lower in fat and cholesterol than comparable cuts of domestic meats. Wild game is truly free-ranging and devoid of antibiotics, steroids and hormones. Properly prepared game dishes will tantalize the senses with rich, intense flavors not found in even the finest quality beef steaks and roasts.

Some of these recipes specify high-fat ingredients such as butter and cream. If you prefer lower-fat dishes, you can achieve similar results by substituting beef or chicken broth or wine combined with a thickening agent. Cornstarch, mixed with an equal amount of cold water, wine or stock will thicken any sauce without adding appreciable amounts of fat or cholesterol. Bring the liquid to a boil and whisk in the cornstarch mixture a little at a time until thickened. A paste made of arrowroot and cold water, added to the sauce while it is still hot, but not boiling, will enable you to achieve similar results.

The addition of fats to game dishes is designed to add moisture to lean meats. Game meats may also be protected from drying out by covering with copious amounts of fresh herbs and vegetables, thus avoiding the addition of high-fat bacon or butter. When preparing a venison roast for example, thinly slice root vegetables such as carrots, potatoes and onions. Lay them over the roast with an assortment of fresh herbs. Not only will you preserve the low-fat benefits of wild game cooking, but you will add flavor and moisture from the herbs and vegetables.

Many of my recipes specify the use of fresh herbs and vegetables. I am fortunate enough to live in an area where fresh herbs and a wide variety of vegetables are in abundance either in my own garden, or at local supermarkets. Should you live in an area where fresh herbs and vegetables are not readily available, it will be necessary to adjust quantities accordingly. Fresh herbs in particular have a distinctly different flavor than dried herbs. Therefore, the finished dish may vary somewhat when dried herbs are substituted for fresh. As a rule of thumb, use about three to four times less quantity of dried herbs when substituting for fresh ones. If you want the very best flavors, consider planting a small herb garden in the sunniest part of your yard during the summer. Herbs are typically hardy and require little care. They can easily be grown in a sunny location indoors in pots as well. You'll want to avoid growing herbs in pots outdoors in direct sun since the soil would dry out quickly and stress the plants. Harvested fresh herbs can be washed, dried and vacuum packaged in FoodSaver VacLoc bags, and stored in your freezer. You can also use zip lock type bags, but watch out for freezer burn. Make sure if you use the zip lock instead of the vacuum bags to push as much air out as possible before sealing the bag. Your fresh herbs will keep for a long time in the vacuum bags. The flavors are in the natural oils of the herb and are superior in flavor to dried herbs.

It is advisable to avoid buying the least expensive ingredients, unless they are available in good quality. I have discovered that lesser-grade cooking products such as inexpensive olive oil or soy sauce often result in an unremarkable meal. If a product is available in a "low-salt" version, buy it. You can always add more salt, but it takes a miracle to reverse an oversalted dish.

Camp Cooking: At Camp and in Your Home.

Without sounding trite, cooking is cooking, unless you're using the wrong equipment. Then it can become drudgery. In this book, you will see me mention the Camp Chef™ Stove numerous times. I also mention FoodSaver®, the home vacuum packaging system. I recommend these two items because I use them. The Camp Chef™ Stove will give you 30,000 BTUs of heat, which will permit you to cook your game quickly, permitting you hold most of the juices and the great wild game flavors inside the meat. It's the heat, the portability, the ease of use that has drawn me to the Camp Chef™, and as I've already mentioned, it's the ability to preserve game for longer periods of time that has drawn me to FoodSaver®. I have arranged for two non-obligation mailer cards at the end of this book for you to use. Mail them in and these fine people will send you more information about their great products.

What If Wild Game Is Not Available?

All recipes in this book can be adapted wonderfully for cooking with non-game meats. Since game meat is a bit more dense, (less fat) you should increase the quantity of meat by about ten percent when using beef, pork and poultry. It will shrink more than game animals due to the increased fat content. Substitute chicken, game hens or commercially-raised rabbit for upland game recipes. Beef will work well with any of the antlered game recipes, and lean trimmed pork will suffice as a substitution for wild boar. I have provided a short list of exchanges at the end of this introduction.

You will discover that I have a penchant for garlic. Game and garlic work together like a hunter and a good bird dog. Although the flavor is not nearly as pronounced, you can substitute minced garlic found in jars, for fresh garlic cloves. In many areas, peeled garlic cloves may be purchased at supermarkets and specialty stores. To peel a fresh garlic clove, set it on a firm flat surface. Place the flat side of a chef's wide blade knife on the garlic and give the knife a firm rap directly above the clove. The skin will peel easily. To mince garlic, repeat the procedure with the chef's knife, except now, you'll want to smash down on the knife with a little more force to flatten the clove. Use the knife to chop up the smashed garlic. Then, sell your garlic press at the next yard sale.

Innovative wild game and non-game preparation requires the cook to invoke the spirit of the pioneer. Go forth boldly into the kitchen and throw caution to the wind. Mix and match flavors with reckless abandon. I am quite certain that our early settlers learned to eat a great many previously unknown animals, fish and plants, prepared in seemingly unorthodox ways, as they made their way across virgin America.

Armed with a good quality chef's knife, a boning knife, and a variety of sauce pans, skillets, roasting pans and stock pots, you're well-prepared to attack magnificent game preparation with the same tenacity that was employed to bag your game. Make liberal use of good wine, fresh herbs and seasonal fruits and vegetables. Experience, creativity, and experimentation will pave the way for you to become a more confident sporting chef.

SUBSTITUTIONS YOU CAN MAKE FOR THE RECIPES IN THIS BOOK

UPLAND GAME

Wild Turkey, whole	Domestic turkey, not pre basted
Wild Turkey, pieces	2 Quartered pheasants
	4 Chukar or Hungarian Partridges
	Domestic turkey pieces, skin, fat removed
Pheasant, whole	2 grouse
	2 Chukar or Hungarian Partridges
	Small domestic turkey, fat removed
Pheasant, cutup	Wild turkey legs and thighs
	4 grouse, quartered
	4 Chukar or Hungarian partridges, quartered
	8 to 12 quail breasts
	Domestic turkey legs and thighs
	Chicken legs and thighs
Quail	Pheasant, cut up
	Ruffed grouse
	Chukar
	Chicken, skin, fat removed
Dove	Quail breasts
	Pheasant, cut up
	Chukar, cut up
Cottontail Rabbit	Squirrels
	Parts of domestic rabbit
	Pheasant or one of its substitutes

BIG GAME

Elk, Caribou	Moose, tenderloin
	Venison, loin portion
	Lean Beef, sirloin, fat removed
Venison	Moose, Elk or Caribou, usually the tenderloin portions
	Lean Beef tenderloin, fat removed
Boar	Shoulder roast from any big game
	Rib roast from moose or elk
	Lean domestic pork tenderloin, fat removed

WEIGHTS AND MEASURES
Used In This Book

3 teaspoons = 1 tablespoon
2 tablespoons = 1 fluid ounce
4 tablespoons = 1/4 cup
8 ounces = 1 cup
1 pint = 2 cups (or 16 fluid ounces)
1 quart = 2 pints (or 32 fluid ounces)
1 gallon = 4 quarts (or 128 fluid Ounces)

STARTERS

I cannot think of a better way to begin a wild game dinner than with a tempting wild game appetizer or salad. A well-prepared first course whets the appetite for the main course to follow. Appetizers can be served in portions at tableside or on platters while partaking of a glass of good wine as the chef puts the finishing touches on the entrée. For a casual dinner, prepare an assortment of appetizers in place of a single main dish.

Many of the main dishes found elsewhere in this book make suitable appetizers. For example, prepare Mallard Breast Stuffed with Mushrooms and Gorgonzola Cheese (see page 20) as per the recipe. Cut the finished rolled breasts into thirds and skewer with a toothpick. Small upland birds such as quail and dove make excellent finger food and can be served right off the grill at game barbecues.

When serving appetizers, make an effort to present them in an attractive manner. Garnish with a sprig of fresh herbs or a thin slice of a colorful vegetable. Avoid serving starter courses in large quantities as you will want your guests to comfortably enjoy the main course.

Photo at left is from the recipe on page 14.
Pan-Fried Quail and Nectarine Salad

7

ASIAN RABBIT MINI-CALZONE

Although you may make four large entrée- sized calzones with this recipe,
I prefer the miniature version as a unique appetizer. Substitute upland game birds, if desired.

Serves - 12

1	pizza dough (see page 9)
¼	cup sesame seeds, lightly toasted in a 325° F oven
½	cup fresh cilantro, minced
2	cups boneless rabbit, cut into 1/2 inch cubes
1	tablespoon cornstarch
2	tablespoons soy sauce
2	tablespoons dry sherry
1	tablespoon seasoned rice vinegar or white wine vinegar sweetened with a pinch of sugar
1	garlic clove, minced
1	tablespoon peanut oil
⅔	cup snow peas, strings and ends removed and sliced into fourths
1	cup mung bean or soy bean sprouts
2	teaspoons fresh ginger, minced
¼	cup red bell pepper, diced
1	cup fresh mushrooms, sliced thinly
⅔	cup fresh or canned pineapple, diced
½	cup apricot preserves
1 ½	cups Monterey Jack cheese, grated

Prepare dough as per recipe, but add sesame seeds and cilantro before mixing.

Combine rabbit with next 5 ingredients, toss and marinate 15 minutes at room temperature. Strain rabbit from marinade. Reserve marinade. In a skillet or wok over medium-high heat, heat peanut oil and add rabbit pieces. Cook until medium brown. Add marinade and cook 2 - 3 minutes more, bringing to a boil. Remove from heat & cool. Place cooked rabbit in a large bowl with remaining ingredients.

Once dough has risen, knead on a lightly floured surface for 2 minutes and form into a roll. Cut roll into 12 equal portions. Roll or press each piece into a 4 inch circle. Place an equal amount of filling into each dough circle and fold over, turning up edges with your fingers to seal in contents. Arrange calzones on a metal sheet pan and place in a pre-heated 450 degree oven for 6 to 8 minutes or until golden brown.

BARBECUED DUCK PIZZA

The variations possible for this appetizer are limited only by your imagination. Experiment with other game meats, cheeses and other toppings to add a personal touch to your pizza.

6 - 8 servings

- 2 large duck breast halves, skin removed and sliced diagonally into very thin strips
- 2 cups tomato-based barbecue sauce
- 2 tablespoons red wine vinegar
- 4 tablespoons olive oil
- 2 garlic cloves, minced
- 4 ounces spicy Italian sausage, casing removed and crumbled
- ¼ portion pizza dough (see right)
- 1 cup gruyére or swiss cheese, grated
- 1 cup parmesan cheese, freshly grated
- 1 cup mozzarella cheese, grated
- ¼ red onion, cut into thin rings
- 4 roma tomatoes, cut into about 5 slices each
- ¼ cup fresh cilantro, chopped

Combine barbecue sauce and vinegar, place in a container with the sliced duck and mix well. Cover and refrigerate for 4 to 6 hours. In a large skillet over medium-high heat, heat 2 tablespoons of the olive oil, add garlic and cook for 1 minute. Add duck with sauce and cook for 3 to 4 minutes, or until duck is just cooked and still tender. Remove duck, set aside to cool and add sausage. Cook until well browned and remove from heat.

Place the dough on a pizza pan, prick several times with a fork and brush with remaining olive oil. Spread cheeses and then duck and sausage evenly over pizza. Top with tomatoes and onion rings. Bake in a 500° oven for 12 to 15 minutes or until crust is golden brown. Sprinkle cilantro over pizza and slice.

Pizza Dough
Makes two 12 inch pizza crusts

- 1 pkg active dry yeast
- 1 cup warm water mixed with 1 tablespoon sugar
- 3 cups all-purpose flour
- 1 teaspoon salt
- ⅛ cup olive oil

In a large mixing bowl, sprinkle yeast over water and stir until dissolved. Place in a warm location for 5 minutes to activate yeast. Add remaining ingredients, one at a time, mixing in each. Place dough on a floured surface and knead until smooth and elastic. Form into a ball, brush top with a little olive oil and place in a greased bowl. Cover and set in a draft-free, warm location for about 1 1/2 hours or until dough has doubled. Shells may be frozen by cooking at 325° for 10 minutes before cooling, wrapping and placing in freezer.

DUCK LEGS CORNELL

Inspired by my long time hunting buddy and business partner, Greg Cornell, during a fundraiser for the California Waterfowl Asoociation. Remove duck legs and freeze them throughout the season until you have enough for this unbelievably tender appetizer.

5 - 8 servings

25-30	assorted duck legs and thighs, skin intact
2	cups pineapple juice
1	cup soy sauce
½	cup cider vinegar
6	garlic cloves, minced
1	tablespoon Tabasco sauce
2	teaspoons chili flakes
½	teaspoon ground dried ginger
1	tablespoon coarse grind black pepper
2	tablespoons sesame seeds
1 ½	cups brown sugar

Pre-heat oven to 450°. Spray a deep baking pan with pan coating spray, then place legs in pan. Combine remaining ingredients and pour over legs. Cover with lid or foil and place in oven. Bake for 1 hour and then rearrange legs in pan. Repeat after baking one more hour. Check legs every 20 minutes or until meat almost falls off of the bone. Remove from pan, place on a serving tray, sprinkle with sesame seeds and allow to cool slightly before serving.

Note: Oven temperatures vary. As the legs cook, the liquid will cook off and thicken. Don't allow the liquid to completely cook off or the legs, and your baking pan, will burn. Add additional liquid if necessary.

ELK CARPACCIO

You will get a true appreciation for the choicest cut of elk by sampling a lightly marinated slice or two of raw tenderloin. Even if you shy away from raw meat, you owe it to yourself to try just a bite.

4 servings

12	ounces elk tenderloin, carefully trimmed of all fat and sinew and sliced paper thin with a very sharp thin-bladed knife or electric slicer.

NOTE: Before slicing, place the meat in the freezer until very cold, but not frozen. You should be able to get at least 12 slices from a 12 ounce tenderloin.

2	tablespoons freshly squeezed lemon juice
2	tablespoons extra virgin olive oil
1	tablespoon red wine vinegar
1	garlic clove
1	tablespoon freshly ground black pepper
2	tablespoons fresh basil, minced

Arrange equal portions of sliced meat on 4 plates. Combine remaining ingredients and drizzle over meat. Let stand 3 to 4 minutes before serving.

ENSALADA AY CARAMBA

This spicy salad calls for rabbit, but the dish works equally well with light-fleshed game birds such as quail, chukar or pheasant.

4 servings

- 2   cottontail rabbits, boned and cut into 1/2 inch cubes
- 2   tablespoons fresh lime juice
- 2   tablespoons fresh lemon juice
- 3   tablespoons tequila
- 1   teaspoon sugar
- 1   tablespoon chili flakes
- 1   tablespoon ground cumin
- ½   teaspoon cayenne pepper
- ½   cup peanut oil
- 2   large corn tortillas, cut into 1/4 inch strips
- 1   medium head iceberg lettuce, shredded
- 1   ripe, but firm avocado, sliced into 12 slices
- 1   cup cooked black beans
- ½   cup sliced black olives
- ½   cup pepper Jack cheese, grated
- 2   cups pico de gallo salsa (see page 88)
- ¼   cup sour cream blended with
- 1   teaspoon fresh lime juice

In a medium bowl, combine rabbit with the next seven ingredients. Cover and marinate in refrigerator for 2 hours, turning 2 or 3 times. Remove rabbit from marinade and drain. In a large skillet over medium-high heat, heat 3 tablespoons of the oil and cook rabbit pieces until well-browned and fully cooked, about 5 minutes. Remove rabbit and set aside to cool. Add remaining oil. When oil is hot, add tortilla strips and cook until crisp. Drain on paper towels.

For each salad, on a large plate, arrange a layer of lettuce, then evenly distribute black beans and olives. Place a small mound of rabbit on the center of the lettuce. Arrange 3 slices of avocado around base of rabbit mound. Mound salsa on rabbit. Place a dollop of sour cream on salsa mound. Distribute cheese evenly and garnish with tortilla strips.

MARINATED GOOSE
WITH CITRUS AND HERB VINAIGRETTE

Those who shy away from the distinctive flavor of goose will be pleasantly surprised with this delightful first course.

6 servings

- 2   Canada geese breast halves, skin removed and sliced diagonally across the "grain" into 1/4 inch strips
- 1   cup olive oil
- ¼   cup orange juice
- 2   tablespoons lime juice
- ½   cup white wine vinegar
- 2   garlic cloves, minced
- 3   tablespoons red onion, minced
- ¼   cup sugar
- ¼   cup fresh basil, minced
- 3   tablespoons fresh oregano, minced
- 2   tablespoons fresh mint, minced
- 1   teaspoon salt
- 1   teaspoon ground mustard
- ½   teaspoon freshly ground black pepper
- 4   cups green cabbage, shredded
- 2   cups red cabbage, shredded
- 1   tablespoon caraway seeds
- 6   slices from a large ripe tomato

In a large skillet or wok over medium-high flame or setting, heat 3 tablespoons of the oil and stir-fry goose until just rare. Remove goose from oil and drain well on paper towels. In a large bowl, combine remaining olive oil and next 12 ingredients. Mix well. Add goose to bowl, toss well, cover and refrigerate for 12 to 24 hours, tossing occasionally.

Remove goose from marinade and form into six mounds. Combine green and red cabbage and caraway seeds and toss with marinade. Place equal portion of cabbage on each plate. Place tomato slice on the center of the cabbage and top with marinated goose.

GRILLED PHEASANT SALAD

A delicious main course salad in the fall or winter when navel oranges are available.

4 servings

4   pheasant breast halves, skin intact
½   teaspoon ground coriander
½   teaspoon dried basil flakes
2   tablespoons honey
½   cup orange juice
1   tablespoon soy sauce
2   teaspoons balsamic vinegar
4   tablespoons brown sugar
4   teaspoons water
⅓   cup slivered almonds
½   medium red onion, peeled and sliced into very thin rings
¾   cup navel orange segments, skin removed
1   head butterleaf lettuce, torn into 2 inch pieces
1   head romaine lettuce, hearts only with large leaves torn in half
½   cup balsamic vinaigrette
⅓   cup bleu cheese crumbles

Balsamic Vinaigrette
Makes 1/2 cup

2   tablespoon balsamic vinegar
⅓   cup olive oil
½   teaspoon dijon mustard
⅛   teaspoon black pepper
   pinch salt

In a small jar with a tight-fitting lid, combine all ingredients and shake vigorously. Can be refrigerated for up to 1 week.

Combine dry seasonings, honey, orange juice, soy sauce and vinegar in bowl. Place pheasant breasts in marinade, cover and refrigerate for 3 to 4 hours, turning breasts occasionally.

Grill or barbecue pheasant breasts over medium heat until just cooked. Remove from heat and allow to cool. Once cooled, remove skin and cut breasts into 3/4 inch cubes.

Pre-heat oven to 375°F. In a small, oven-safe non-stick skillet over medium heat, add water, sugar and almonds. Stir frequently while sugar caramelizes and coats almonds. When caramel starts to thicken, place skillet in oven until almonds are lightly browned, spreading out almonds to brown evenly. Remove skillet, let cool. After almonds cool, break up large pieces.

In a large bowl, toss pheasant, almonds and remaining ingredients, reserving a few bleu cheese crumbles. Place equal portion of salad on four plates, topping each with reserved bleu cheese crumbles.

PHEASANT TIMBALES
WITH LEMON VINAIGRETTE

A delightful appetizer with extraordinary flavor and eye appeal. Serve with baby lettuces for a delicious salad.

6 servings

- 2 pheasant breast halves, skin removed, poached in chicken broth, cooled and hand-pulled into small strips
- 1 large red bell pepper, roasted, peeled, seeded and cut into 6 strips (see page 87 for directions for roasting bell pepper)
- 2 cups fresh spinach, steamed for 1 minute and drained well on paper towels
- ½ cup feta cheese, crumbled
- 1 cup half and half
- 2 large eggs
- 2 tablespoons butter
- 1 tablespoon shallot or green onion bulb, minced
- 2 tablespoons red wine vinegar
- 1 teaspoon dijon mustard
- juice of 1 lemon
- ⅓ cup olive oil
- 1 egg white
- *salt and pepper*
- 2 cups green or Nappa cabbage, shredded
- 1 medium tomato, seeded and diced into 1/4 inch cubes

For vinaigrette, combine shallot, vinegar, mustard and lemon in a medium bowl. While whisking, add oil in a thin stream and then egg white. Whisk until emulsified. Season with salt and pepper.

Bring the half and half to a boil in a sauce pan over medium-high heat. Lightly season with salt and pepper. In a bowl, beat the eggs, and then whisk the hot half and half into the eggs. Add the cheese and stir to blend. Grease 6 individual ramekins or 6 sections of a muffin tin with the butter. Fill each ramekin with equal amounts of cheese, half and half and egg mixture, making sure that the cheese is equally distributed. Lay equal amounts of well-drained spinach in ramekin, followed by red bell pepper and shredded pheasant. Liquid should "bleed" throughout ramekin. Place timbales in a baking dish filled with water 1/2 inch below the rim of ramekins. Bake in a 350°F oven for 30 minutes. Remove from oven and run a sharp knife around the inside of the ramekin and remove timbales. On six plates, distribute cabbage, place one timbale on each portion of cabbage and drizzle over with vinaigrette. Top with diced tomato.

13

PAN-FRIED QUAIL
AND NECTARINE SALAD

Quail season starts early while you can still take advantage of late- season nectarines.
Peaches may be substituted for nectarines if they are more plentiful in your part of the country.

4 servings

6	quail, skin intact and cut in half
¼	cup dry sherry
½	cup flour
1	teaspoon garlic powder
½	teaspoon salt
¼	teaspoon black pepper
¼	teaspoon dried basil flakes
½	teaspoon paprika
¾	cup vegetable oil
4	handfulls mixed baby lettuce or a mixture of red leaf, butter leaf and romaine lettuce, if baby lettuce is unavailable
1	cup dry roasted and salted peanuts
¼	cup medium red onion, peeled and diced fine
1 ½	cups celery, diced
1	cup jicama, peeled and julienned
2	ripe, but firm nectarines, cut into wedges

Dressing

1	each egg white
¼	cup seasoned rice vinegar
¼	cup peach preserves
1	each garlic clove, minced
2	teaspoons dijon mustard
	juice of 1 lemon
¼	cup sour cream
¼	cup olive oil
	salt and pepper to taste

Place above ingredients except oil, salt and pepper in a blender or food processor and blend until smooth. While blending, add olive oil in a thin steady stream until emulsified. Season with salt and pepper.

Soak quail in sherry for 20 minutes, turning often. In a plastic bag, combine the next 6 ingredients. Place quail in bag to coat with seasonings and flour. In a large, heavy skillet over medium-high heat, heat oil until hot. Brown quail evenly on each side, about 2 - 3 minutes per side. Remove quail and set on paper towels to drain excess oil.

In a large bowl, toss remaining ingredients, reserving a little dressing. Arrange salad mixture on 4 large plates and distribute 3 quail halves per plate. Drizzle remaining dressing over quail. (See photo pg. 6)

PHEASANT TEMPURA

*Great finger food to begin a game feast with an Asian flair.
Choose your favorite vegetables and serve with an assortment
of dipping sauces such as Plum Sauce (see page 89) or Chinese
Hot Mustard.*

6 - 8 servings

Batter
    4   eggs
  2 ⅔ cups flour
    2   teaspoons   salt
    2   cups flat beer

Preparation
    2   boneless pheasant breast halves, skin removed and
         sliced diagonally into 1/2 inch thick strips
    2   carrots, peeled and cut into 1/2 inch by 3 inch
         sticks
    2   zucchini, cut into 1/2 inch by 3 inch sticks
   10   fresh mushrooms, whole
    1   large red bell pepper, cut lengthwise into 8 strips
    1   quart peanut oil

To prepare batter, beat eggs in a bowl and then add 2/3 cup
flour and salt. Add beer and remaining flour, a little of each at
a time, beating after each addition. Do not overbeat. Batter
should be a little lumpy. Allow batter to stand for 1 hour.

Heat oil in wok, deep fryer or deep sauce pan to about 375° F.

Using tongs or chopsticks, dip each piece in batter, fry both
sides until golden brown and serve immediately.

GRILLED VENISON SKEWERS
WITH DIPPING SAUCE

*Grilling time is critical as prolonged cooking will result in something
more closely resembling beef jerky. Any antlered game will suffice.*

6 - 8 servings (20 skewers)

  2 ½   pounds venison top round or rump roast,
          sliced across the grain into 1/4 inch thick
          strips (about 2 ounces each)

***Note: Slicing with the grain will make the skewers
chewier***

    ½   cup Worcestershire sauce
    ½   cup game stock or beef broth
    ¼   cup soy sauce
    2   tablespoons balsamic vinegar
    4   garlic cloves, minced
    2   tablespoons cracked black pepper
         (or 1 tablespoon table ground)
   20   bamboo skewers, soaked for 30
          minutes in water
    2   cups Mustard Dipping Sauce (see page 89)

Combine Worcestershire sauce, game stock, soy sauce,
vinegar, garlic and pepper in a large bowl. Add sliced
venison, mix well, cover and marinate in refrigerator for 3
to 4 hours, turning occasionally. Remove meat and skewer
lengthwise on bamboo skewers. Place on a well-greased
barbecue over white-hot coals and sear on each side, about
2 minutes per side. Arrange on a platter around a bowl of
dipping sauce.

SMOKED DUCK TOASTS
WITH RED CHILI AIOLI

A tempting appetizer with a spicy hot finish.

24 - 28 toasts

1	large smoked duck, breast meat only (see page 73)
6-8	thin slices sourdough or rye bread
½	cup olive oil
6	garlic cloves, minced
½	teaspoon chili flakes
¼	teaspoon salt
1	egg yolk at room temperature
2	teaspoons fresh lemon juice
2	teaspoons fresh lime juice
½	teaspoon cayenne pepper
1	teaspoon chili powder
⅔	cup olive oil
24-28	fresh cilantro leaves

Slice breasts diagonally across the grain into very thin strips. Combine next three ingredients and brush one side of bread slices. Trim crusts and cut bread into 4 triangles per slice. Lay triangles on a sheet pan and toast in a 325° F oven until lightly browned. In a food processor or blender, combine next 6 ingredients and process until blended. While processor is running, add oil in a very thin stream until aioli thickens. Spoon a small dollop of the aioli on the center of each toast. Fold each duck slice to fit the toast and place the folded slices on the aioli. Garnish each with a fresh cilantro leaf.

RUFFED GROUSE
A LA RUBIO

Dedicated to my boyhood hunting companion, Steve Rubio, with whom I walked miles of logging roads in the Blue Ridge Mountains in pursuit of this elusive bird. Also great served as a main dish with wild rice.

6 - 8 servings

8	ruffed grouse, boned, and cut into bite-sized pieces
1	tablespoon freshly ground black pepper
1	teaspoon onion powder
¼	teaspoon salt
2	tablespoons olive oil
½	cup dry white wine
3	garlic cloves, minced
2	medium zucchini, diced
1	medium carrot, diced
1	large russet potato, peeled and diced
1	tablespoon green peppercorns
1	tablespoon fresh rosemary, minced
1	cup game bird or chicken stock
1	large ripe tomato, peeled, seeded and quartered
2	green onions, diced
1	tablespoon cornstarch mixed with equal part cold water *(optional)*
	salt and freshly ground pepper to taste

Season grouse with next 3 ingredients. Heat oil in a large skillet over medium-high heat and brown grouse evenly. Remove grouse, add wine and cook until liquid is reduced by one-half. Add garlic, vegetables and peppercorns; cook 3 -4 minutes. Add rosemary and stock, bring to boil, reduce heat low and simmer, uncovered, for 15 minutes. Add grouse, tomato and green onions. Simmer 5 minutes more. Thicken with cornstarch mixture, a little at a time, if desired. Season with salt and pepper.

FoodSaver

"I mention vacuum packaging your game more than once. The best vacuum packaging system I know of, comes from FoodSaver. The FoodSaver people were kind enough to offer you a real savings special if you call 1-800 777 5452 and mention this book. This is one product you will never regret buying." - Scott Leysath

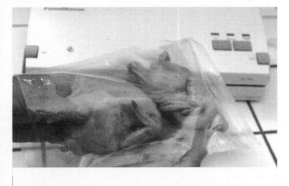

Place item(s) to be sealed into VacLoc™ Bag.

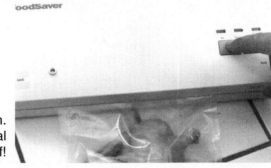

Press and hold "On" switch. FoodSaver will vacuum, seal and turn itself off!

Lay edge of bag in trough. Make sure edge lies flat.

To seal before a complete vacuum has been pulled, simply press the "Manual" seal button.

Close unit. Rubber pressure pads will hold bag in place.

Open lid and remove bag. It's that easy!

WATERFOWL

During a recent pre-dawn hike through a 70-mile-per-hour rain storm -- so that I could reach a strategically located duck blind in a flooded rice field in northern California -- I was reminded of why I truly love the outdoor experience. While non-hunters may question the sanity of anyone who would seek out such "pleasures" voluntarily, those who have been bombarded by countless ducks in a fierce storm, fully comprehend my affinity for waterfowl hunting. According to labor statistics, nasty weather during duck season is a major contributor to employee attendance problems. Is it any wonder?

If you're not inclined to brave gale force winds, you can purchase commercially raised waterfowl in many markets or from a few 1-800 services.

Armed with a wine glass full of a robust cabernet sauvignon, a skillet and a few select ingredients, you can cook a wild duck that will rival its portly commercially-raised cousin usually found in

Photo at left is from the recipe on page 24.
Duck Ravioli with Lemon Cream Sauce

our nation's finest restaurants. While I have enjoyed several slow-roasted ducks in years past, my favorite method of waterfowl cooking is perhaps the easiest. Start with a hot skillet, add olive oil and fresh garlic. Brown both sides of a pair of duck breasts. Add wine, fresh rosemary, fresh earthy mushrooms, a little butter, salt and pepper and *presto*, a perfectly prepared duck!

The above described technique for cooking ducks specifies duck breasts. While the breasts can best be cooked quickly, legs and thighs require extended cooking to break down the fibrous tendons. I prefer to separate legs and thighs from wild waterfowl and cook separately or use for making stocks. (See: Duck Legs Cornell, Page 10).

Historically, many duck recipes call for the stuffing of the cavity with an assortment of fruits and vegetables. I have yet to taste any discernable flavors with this practice, but I suppose it may help to somewhat prevent drying out the finished bird. Stuffing whole birds will require extended cooking times to cook the meat close to the rib cage, therefore, it should be discouraged.

When wild ducks and geese are in short supply, try these recipes with lean cuts of pork, poultry and veal.

MALLARD BREAST STUFFED
WITH MUSHROOMS & GORGONZOLA CHEESE

*An elegant dish for a special occasion when
you really want to impress your guests.*

4 servings

4-6	mallard breast halves, skin removed
¼	cup flour
¼	teaspoon white pepper
½	teaspoon garlic powder
1	pinch salt
4	tablespoons butter
1	tablespoon olive oil
¼	cup dry sherry
3	cups mushrooms, sliced thin
1	garlic clove, minced
6	ounces gorgonzola cheese, crumbled
1	tablespoon fresh parsley, minced
	salt and freshly ground black pepper

Place duck breasts between waxed paper sheets and pound lightly with the flat side of a mallet until meat is 1/4 inch thick or as thin as possible without tearing flesh. Flour 1 side of each breast. In a large skillet, over medium-high flame, heat 2 tablespoons of the butter and brown on the floured side only, about 1 to 2 minutes each breast. Remove breasts, de-glaze pan with sherry, add olive oil and 1 tablespoon butter. Sauté mushrooms and garlic for 2 minutes. Remove from heat. Lay out breasts, browned side down and place equal amount of cheese on the bottom third of each. Spoon 1/4 cup of mushrooms over cheese and begin rolling by grasping the bottom edge of the breast and folding over cheese and mushroom mixture, keeping stuffing in with your fingers. Roll snugly and place, "seam" side down, in a baking dish. Place rolled breasts in a 400° F oven for 6 to 8 minutes, or until cheese begins to run out. Meanwhile, return skillet to medium heat. Add parsley and cook for 3 minutes more. Remove from heat, stir in remaining 1 tablespoon of butter and season with salt and pepper. Place one breast on each plate and spoon mushrooms over each.

MU SHU GOOSE

Pronounced Asian flavors combine with stir-fried goose for a delicious and unorthodox game dish. Don't forget the Boar Fried Rice (see page 78). Pancake Recipe used with this recipe can be found on Page 27.

4 servings

10	dried black mushrooms, soaked in hot water for 20 minutes, stems removed & caps sliced thin.
4	tablespoons peanut oil
2	eggs, lightly beaten
1	Canada goose breast, both halves, skin removed and cut into matchstick-sized strips
1	garlic clove, minced
½	teaspoon fresh ginger, minced
1	cup sliced bamboo shoots, drained
2	cups green cabbage, shredded
1	medium carrot, shredded
3	green onions with tops, cut into 1/2 inch pieces
2	teaspoons soy sauce
2	teaspoons dry sherry
1	teaspoon sesame oil
½	pound bean sprouts
¼	cup hoisin sauce
8	Chinese pancakes (see page 27)

Heat 2 tablespoons oil in a wok or large skillet over medium-high setting. Add eggs and cook until just set. Remove eggs, break apart and set aside. Add remaining oil, heat and stir-fry garlic and ginger 1 minute. Add goose, cook 2 minutes. Add mushrooms, bamboo shoots, cabbage, carrots, onions, soy sauce, sherry and sesame oil. Stir-fry 1 minute. Add bean sprouts and eggs and cook 30 seconds to warm. Spread a thin layer of hoisin sauce over each pancake and roll with goose filling.

DUCK
WITH RASPBERRY SAUCE

Served with plenty of raspberry sauce, this dish is an excellent
one to initiate those who think they don't like game.

4 servings

- 4 - 6 large duck breast halves, skin intact
- 4 garlic cloves, minced
- 1 tablespoon freshly ground black pepper
- 2 teaspoons fresh rosemary, minced
- ¼ teaspoon salt
- 2 tablespoons brown sugar
- 2 tablespoons raspberry liqueur
- 2 tablespoons butter
- 1 tablespoon olive oil
- ¼ cup dry red wine
- 1 cup raspberry sauce (86)
- ½ cup fresh raspberries, if available

In a small bowl, combine garlic, pepper, rosemary, salt, sugar and liqueur. Rinse duck breasts with cold water and pat dry with paper towels. Rub seasoning mixture over duck breasts, cover and refrigerate for 4 hours.

In a large skillet heat oil and butter over medium-high flame. Place duck breasts, skin side down in hot butter and oil and cook until skin side is medium brown, about 4 minutes. Flip breasts over and cook other side 3 to 4 minutes more, or until breasts feel just rare. Add wine, cook for 2 to 3 more minutes. Remove duck breasts and let stand for 3 to 4 minutes. Slice diagonally and fan equal portions on each plate. Spoon raspberry sauce over half of each portion and garnish with fresh raspberries.

MALLARD STIR-FRY
WITH MANDARIN ORANGES

Cook it fast and hot for remarkable flavors! Serve with steamed
white rice and cold Asian beer.

4 servings

- 3 - 4 mallard breasts, skin removed and sliced into 1/4 inch thick strips
- 2 tablespoons cold water
- 1 ½ tablespoons cornstarch
- 2 tablespoons soy sauce
- ¼ teaspoon sesame oil
- 2 tablespoons seasoned rice vinegar
- 2 tablespoons soy sauce
- 2 garlic cloves, minced
- 2 tablespoons peanut oil
- ½ medium red bell pepper, cut in thin strips
- ½ medium green bell pepper, cut in thin strips
- ¼ medium red onion, cut in thin strips
- 1 teaspoon fresh ginger, minced
- 1 tablespoon brown sugar
- 1 ounce canned Mandarin orange segments

In a medium bowl, mix cornstarch and water. Add the next 5 ingredients and toss with duck breast strips. Cover and refrigerate for 1 hour.

In a wok or heavy-duty deep skillet over high heat, add oil. When oil is hot, add peppers, onion and ginger. Stir-fry 1 to 2 minutes. Add duck, marinade mixture and brown sugar. Stir-fry 3 minutes. Reduce heat to low, add Mandarin orange segments and cook 1 minute more.

GLAZED PEKING-STYLE DUCK

Save this recipe for a pair of large carefully plucked ducks with no breaks in the skin of the breast. Great with steamed rice and stir-fried fresh vegetables.

4 servings

2   whole mallard, canvasback or black ducks, skin and neck intact (add an additional duck
     if your guests have particularly hearty appetites)
1   cup coffee liqueur
¼   cup grenadine syrup
¼   cup honey
2   teaspoons fresh ginger, peeled and minced
2   garlic cloves, minced
¼   cup orange juice
¼   teaspoon five-spice powder (optional)
⅓   cup orange juice
¼   cup hoisin sauce
3   tablespoons soy sauce
1   teaspoon sesame oil
1   tablespoon cornstarch mixed with 1 T cold water

Wash ducks thoroughly with cold water and pat dry with paper towels. Combine next 6 ingredients and pour over ducks in a shallow container. Marinate ducks in refrigerator for 12 hours, turning often to coat evenly. Remove ducks, draining liquid into container with remaining marinade. Pour marinade into a container and reserve.

Tie a cord around the neck of each duck and hang in a cool, dry, well- ventilated area for 4 hours. Place ducks, breast side down on a rack in a roasting pan and bake in a pre-heated 450°F oven for 15 minutes, basting with half of reserved marinade two or three times during cooking. Turn ducks breast side up, baste one more time and bake for 6 to 8 more minutes or until skin is crisp and meat is firm, but still moist. Internal temperature of the duck should not exceed 140°F. Remove duck from pan and let stand for 5 to 8 minutes.

While pan is still warm, carefully add orange juice and scrape pan to loosen any bits of duck or marinade. Add liquid to a medium sauce pan with remaining marinade, hoisin, soy sauce and sesame oil. Heat to boil and thicken with cornstarch mixture, if necessary.

Carve breasts from rib cage, leaving the skin intact. Slice diagonally into 1/4 inch slices. Remove legs and thighs. On a large platter, arrange sliced breasts, legs and thighs. Pour sauce into small bowls for dipping.

HOLIDAY DUCK
WITH BURGUNDY AND CRANBERRY SAUCE

Forego the turkey on Thanksgiving and try this refreshing duck dish.

6 servings

- 12 large duck breast halves, skin intact
- 4 cups burgundy wine
- 2 tablespoons Worcestershire sauce
- 4 fresh rosemary sprigs
- ½ medium onion, coarse chopped
- 4 garlic cloves, minced
- 2 tablespoons cracked black pepper
- 2 tablespoons olive oil
- 3 tablespoons shallots, chopped
- 1 ½ cups fresh or frozen cranberries
- ¼ cup honey
- 4 ounces butter, cut into 4 pieces
- *salt and pepper*

In a large bowl, combine 2 cups wine, Worcestershire sauce, rosemary, onion and half of the minced garlic. Place duck breasts in marinade, cover and refrigerate for 6 to 8 hours. Turn duck 2 or 3 times while marinating. Remove ducks, pat dry with paper towels. Pour marinade into a medium sauce pan over medium-high heat. Add shallots and remaining wine. Reduce to approximately 1 1/2 cups of liquid. Pour through strainer and return strained liquid to sauce pan. Add cranberries and honey, reduce heat to medium-low and cook for 10 minutes or until cranberries soften. Remove from heat.

Rub reserved garlic over breasts and coat with pepper. In a large skillet over medium-high heat, brown breasts on both sides (skin side first), about 4 minutes per side. Add 1/2 cup of the sauce and cook for 2 minutes more. Remove ducks and let stand 3 to 4 minutes before carving diagonally into 1/4 inch thick slices. Return sauce to heat until bubbling. Remove from heat and whisk in butter sections, one at a time, until sauce thickens. Season with salt and pepper. On a large platter, arrange duck slices and pour sauce over middle of slices. Serve any leftover sauce on the side.

EASY BARBECUED
ORANGE - ROSEMARY DUCK

Add seasoned vegetables and boiled red potatoes to the grill for a complete outdoor repast. This preparation also works well with all upland game.

6 servings

- 12 large to medium duck breast halves, skin intact
- 1 cup dry white wine
- ¼ cup white wine vinegar
- ½ cup soy sauce
- 1 tablespoon pickling spices
- 6 ounces butter, softened
- 2 garlic cloves, minced
- 1 ½ cups orange marmalade
- 1 tablespoon fresh rosemary, minced
- ⅔ cup dry white wine
- *pinch white pepper*

In a large bowl, mix 1 cup wine, vinegar, soy sauce and pickling spices. Place duck breasts in marinade, cover and refrigerate for 24 hours. Pre-heat barbecue coals or gas charbroiler to medium-hot. Combine remaining ingredients. Place breasts on grill, skin side down. Baste with sauce. Cook 4 minutes per side or until breast meat is just firm to finger pressure, basting frequently. Top with any leftover sauce and serve immediately.

23

DRUNKEN DUCK BREASTS

As the name implies, the duck breasts are marinated and then cooked in generous amounts of alcohol. Cheers!

4 servings

8	medium to large duck breast halves, skin intact
1	cup brandy
½	cup triple sec liqueur
¼	cup brown sugar
2	tablespoons freshly squeezed lemon juice
2	tablespoons fresh ginger, grated
2	tablespoon cracked black pepper
3	tablespoons olive oil
1	medium onion, peeled and quartered
½	cup beef broth
3	tablespoons fresh mint, chopped
¼	cup heavy cream
	salt and freshly ground pepper to taste

Rinse duck breasts with cold water and pat dry with paper towels. Combine next 6 ingredients in a non-metallic bowl. Mix well to blend. Add duck breasts, toss to coat, cover and refrigerate for 12 hours, turning occasionally. Remove from marinade, drain well and reserve marinade.

Heat oil in a large heavy skillet over medium-high heat. Place duck breasts, skin side down, and onion into skillet. Cook until skin side is lightly browned, about 3-5 minutes. Flip breasts over and cook other side for an additional 4 minutes or until meat is just rare. Remove breasts and add reserved marinade and beef broth. Cook until liquid is reduced by two-thirds. Reduce heat to medium, stir in chopped mint and cream and heat until sauce thickens, stirring frequently. Season with salt and pepper. Return duck to skillet and heat to serving temperatures. Slice duck breasts and place an equal portion of duck and onion on each plate. Spoon sauce over each portion.

Caution: The marinade contains alcohol and may ignite. Please be careful when adding.

DUCK RAVIOLI
WITH LEMON CREAM SAUCE

Won ton wrappers greatly reduce preparation time

4 - 5 servings

3-5	duck breasts (about 8 ounces), cooked rare, cooled and minced
½	cup ricotta cheese
¼	cup dry Monterey Jack cheese, grated
¼	cup Parmesan cheese, grated
2	garlic cloves, chopped
½	cup fresh basil, chopped
¼	cup green onion, chopped
2	tablespoons sundried tomatoes, in oil, chopped
50	won ton wrappers
1	cup flour
¼	cup cornstarch mixed with 1/4 cup cold water
¼	cup freshly grated Parmesan cheese

Place all of the above ingredients except won ton wrappers and cornstarch mixture in a blender or food processor. Pulse until all ingredients are blended into a coarse paste.

On a flat surface, sift flour evenly over. Lay won ton wrappers out as room allows. Form the filling into discs about the size of a 50 cent piece, about 1/4 inch thick. Place a disc on the center of each of the won ton wrappers. Brush cornstarch mixture evenly around the exposed area of the wrapper. Place a second wrapper, centered over the filling disc, atop the first and press firmly, but carefully, sealing all edges. Repeat process for all wrappers, making a total of 25 ravioli. Sift flour over all exposed surfaces, place on floured waxed paper in a container, cover and place in freezer for at least 2 hours. Ravioli can be prepared several days ahead and frozen indefinitely.

Prepare Lemon Cream Sauce (Page 89). Keep warm. In a large stock pot add water, 2 tablespoons vegetable oil and 1 tablespoon salt. Bring to boil. Reduce heat to low and add ravioli, one at a time, stirring gently to prevent sticking. Cook for 4 to 5 minutes or until ravioli are tender and translucent. Spoon warmed sauce onto plates and top with ravioli and grated Parmesan cheese. (See photo on page 18)

PEPPERCORN DUCK
WITH HORSERADISH SAUCE

Reminiscent of carved prime rib. Serve with roasted new red potatoes seasoned with fresh rosemary and lots of fresh garlic.

4 servings

- 4-6 large duck breast halves, skin intact
- ½ cup whole grain mustard
- ¼ cup brined green peppercorns
- 3 tablespoons pink peppercorns
- 3 tablespoons black peppercorns
- ¼ teaspoons salt
- ¼ cup seasoned bread crumbs
- 3 tablespoons olive oil
- 1 cup béchamel sauce (see page 86) or substitute heavy cream
- ¼ cup prepared horseradish
- 1 teaspoon Worcestershire sauce
- 2 teaspoons fresh chives, fine diced (or substitute green onion tops)

Coat duck breasts evenly with mustard. With a mortar and pestle, combine peppercorns and grind until peppercorns are crushed. Add salt and bread crumbs and mix thoroughly. You may also crush peppercorns under a heavy flat-bottom skillet on a hard surface, pressing down on the skillet, but it can be a bit messy as the peppercorns escape from the pan. Coat the duck breasts with the peppercorn mixture.

Add olive oil to a large skillet over medium-high heat. When oil is hot, add duck breasts and lightly brown on both sides, about 3 to 4 minutes per side. Reduce heat to low, cover skillet and cook for 2 minutes more. Remove from heat and let stand for 5 minutes.

To make sauce, combine béchamel sauce, horseradish and Worcestershire in a small sauce pan and heat until warm. Slice duck breasts very thinly on a diagonal across the "grain" and fan out equal portions on each plate. Spoon sauce over one-half of each breast portion and garnish with chives.

SESAME
CRUSTED DUCK

The sesame crust helps to retain moisture and adds flavor, texture and eye appeal to large duck breasts.

4 servings

- 6-8 mallards, black or canvas back duck breast halves, skin intact
- ½ cup whole grain mustard
- 1 teaspoon freshly ground black pepper
- ½ teaspoon salt
- 1 cup sesame seeds
- 3 tablespoons peanut oil

In a medium bowl, combine pepper, salt and sesame seeds. Coat each breast with mustard. Press each breast evenly into seed mixture, coating both sides with seeds. In a large skillet over medium heat, heat oil and cook each breast on both sides until sesame seeds turn golden brown.

Turn each side gently only once to keep seed crust intact.

Serve immediately.

TEAL SCALOPPINE

It might take more than a few of these fast fliers to feed four adults, but the flavor and tenderness is beyond compare. Try this preparation method for all ducks.

4 servings

15 teal half breasts, skin removed
½ cup flour, seasoned with 1 teaspoon garlic powder,
    1/4 teaspoon pepper, and 1/4 teaspoon salt
3 tablespoons olive oil
2 tablespoons butter
3 garlic cloves, minced
½ medium yellow onion, chopped
½ pound fresh mushrooms, thick sliced
½ cup dry white wine
½ cup game bird or chicken stock
    juice of 1 lemon
2 tablespoons fresh parsley, minced
1 teaspoon flour
½ cup sour cream
¾ cup fresh tomato, peeled, seeded and diced

Place duck breasts between waxed paper sheets and pound with a flat mallet to ¼ inch thick. Dredge each breast in seasoned flour. In a large skillet over medium-high heat, heat 2 tablespoons of the oil and 1 tablespoon of the butter. Place breasts in skillet and lightly brown on both sides, about 1 to 2 minutes per side. Remove breasts and set aside.

Add remaining butter and oil to pan and sauté garlic and onion for 2 minutes. Add wine, chicken stock and lemon juice. Bring to boil, reduce heat to medium and simmer, uncovered, for 6 to 8 minutes or until liquid is reduced by one-half. Add browned duck breasts, mushrooms and parsley, cover and cook for 3 more minutes. Remove breasts and keep warm. Blend remaining flour with sour cream, add to pan and cook, stirring occasionally, until sauce thickens. Place four breasts on each plate, pour equal amount of sauce over each and top with diced tomatoes.

THE TEN MINUTE DUCK

When you're in the mood for duck dinner, but really don't feel like cooking. Grab a skillet, a handful of ingredients and whip up a masterpiece in just ten minutes!

4 servings

4 - 6 large boneless duck breasts,
    skin intact
½ teaspoon freshly ground pepper
½ teaspoon garlic powder
½ teaspoon dried rosemary
¼ teaspoon salt
3 tablespoons olive oil
⅓ cup dry red wine
2 cups mushrooms, sliced
⅓ cup raspberry preserves

Rinse breasts with cold water and pat dry with paper towels. Season with next four ingredients. Heat oil in a large skillet over medium-high heat. Place breasts, skin side down, in skillet and cook until skin is medium brown, about 3 minutes. Flip breasts over and cook 3 minutes more. Add wine and mushrooms and cook 2 minutes. Remove duck from skillet and whisk in preserves for 1 minute. Slice duck breasts, arrange on plate and top with mushrooms and sauce.

Chinese Pancakes

1 cup flour
½ cup boiling water
2 tablespoons sesame oil

In a medium bowl, add flour. Mix in boiling water until dough is formed. Place dough ball on a floured surface and knead for 5 minutes until smooth. Cover with a moistened cloth and let stand for 20 minutes. Knead for 2 minutes more and roll into cylinder. Cut dough into 8 equal pieces and flatten into same-sized pancakes. Brush sesame oil on one side of each. Put two pancakes together, oiled sides touching and roll with a rolling pin until a 6 inch circle is formed. Repeat process with remaining pancakes. In an ungreased non-stick pan over low heat cook pancakes on each side until lightly browned and slightly puffy. Remove and separate pancakes. Place hoisin sauce and filling on oiled side of pancake and roll. (Use with Mu Shu Goose, page 20).

CUMBERLAND DUCK

Pan-seared duck breasts team up with traditional Cumberland sauce for a quick and simple main course.

4 servings

4-6	large to medium duck breast halves, skin intact
1	cup orange juice
3	tablespoons lemon juice
¾	cup port wine
2	tablespoons olive oil
3	strips smoked bacon, diced fine
1	tablespoon shallot, minced
1	rind of 1 orange, white part removed and cut into thin strips
1	rind of 1 lemon, white part removed and cut into thin strips
1	cup red currant jelly
1	tablespoon dijon mustard
1	pinch cayenne pepper
1	pinch ground ginger
1	tablespoon Grand Marnier or orange liqueur
	salt and freshly ground black pepper to taste

Combine lemon and orange juice with 1/2 cup of the wine. Marinate duck breasts for 3 - 4 hours in refrigerator. Turn breasts 3 or 4 times while marinating. In a small sauce pan with boiling water, add sliced lemon and orange rind. Cook for 3 to 4 minutes, remove and plunge into icy water. Reserve blanched rinds.

Remove breasts from marinade. Reserve marinade. Cook diced bacon with oil over medium-high heat for 2 to 3 minutes. Place duck breasts skin side down in skillet, and brown to rare on each side — about 3 to 5 minutes per side — depending on the size of the breasts. Remove breasts, set aside and add reserved marinade, shallots and reserved blanched rind to pan. Reduce liquid by two-thirds. Add duck breasts and all other remaining ingredients except Grand Marnier, salt and pepper. Reduce heat to low and cook, stirring often until jelly is melted. Add 1/4 cup port wine and Grand Marnier. Cook 2 more minutes. Remove duck breasts, let stand for 4 to 5 minutes. Slice thin diagonally across the breast. Season sauce with salt and pepper and spoon equal amount on each plate. Top with sliced duck.

GOOSE LUZIANNE

*Spicy New Orleans style goose best served over white rice.
An exception to the "cook it fast and hot" rule, simmer the goose
long enough for the meat to become tender.*

6 servings

- 3-4 Canada honker or speckled goose breast halves, skin removed and meat cut into half inch cubes
- 1 cup red wine
- ¼ cup red wine vinegar
- 3 tablespoons Worcestershire sauce
- 1 tablespoon freshly ground black pepper
- 1 cup peanut oil
- 1 cup flour
- 2 cups celery, chopped
- 1 cup yellow onion, diced
- 1 cup green bell pepper, diced
- 10 fresh garlic cloves, minced
- 1 teaspoon each cayenne pepper, white pepper, salt and dried basil
- 1 quart game bird or chicken stock
- 1 pound andouille sausage, cut into ½ inch slices and sauteed until lightly browned
- 2 cups fresh oysters and their liquid
- 1 cup fresh tomato, diced

In a non-metallic bowl, combine cubed goose with next 4 ingredients. Toss well, cover and refrigerate for 6-12 hours. Drain and reserve marinade. In a heavy-duty medium stock pot over medium-high heat, heat 2 tablespoons of the oil, add goose and brown pieces evenly. Remove goose and add a little reserved marinade, stirring to remove bits of meat from the pot. Add remaining oil until very hot and carefully add flour, whisking constantly until flour browns, about 20 minutes. Add vegetables, garlic and spices; cook 3 minutes while stirring. Add stock, cooked goose and reserved marinade, bring to boil. reduce heat to low and simmer for 1 hour. Add remaining ingredients and simmer for 5 minutes. Adjust seasonings, if necessary, and serve.

28

LAST CHANCE DUCK BREASTS

*A few birds like Coots or Mergansers may require a little more time and effort
for transformation into great duck dinners. This recipe also works well with
ducks stuck to the back corner of your freezer, just under the muskrat salami
given to you by Uncle Stinky a few years back.*

4 servings

- 6-8 boneless duck breasts. skin removed and cut into thin strips

Marinade

- 10 whole garlic cloves, minced
- ½ cup white wine vinegar
- ½ cup dry white wine
- ½ cup game stock or beef broth
- 3 tablespoons Worcestershire sauce
- 2 tablespoons pickling spices

Preparation

- 2 tablespoons olive oil
- ½ medium yellow onion, diced
- 6 whole garlic cloves, roasted in a 350° F oven until softened and lightly browned
- 1 tablespoon fresh rosemary, minced
- ¼ cup dry white wine
- 1 tablespoon Worcestershire sauce
- 4 ounces butter, chilled and cut into 4 pieces
  salt and freshly ground black pepper to taste

Combine marinade ingredients in a glass or plastic bowl, whisk to blend, add duck and toss to coat thoroughly. Cover and refrigerate for 48 hours.

Remove duck from marinade, drain well. Discard marinade. Heat oil in a large skillet over medium-high heat, add onion and saute for 3 minutes. Add duck and sauté for 3 minutes, stirring to sear all sides. Add next four ingredients. Sauté for 3 minutes more. Move contents to one side of pan. Remove pan from heat and whisk butter into liquid, one piece at a time until melted. Season with salt and pepper.

BARBECUED GOOSE
WITH HERBS AND WINE

The flavor improves dramatically when goose breasts are barbecued over smoky wood, charcoal or wood chips rather than propane. If fresh herbs simply are not available, substitute greatly reduced quantities of dried herbs.

4 servings

2-3	Canada honker or speckled goose boneless breasts
	skin intact
1	teaspoon white pepper
1	tablespoon garlic powder
1	teaspoon salt
1	cup dry white wine
1 ½	cups olive or peanut oil
½	cup white wine vinegar
½	cup fresh basil, chopped
2	tablespoons fresh rosemary, minced
2	tablespoons fresh sage, minced
2	tablespoons fresh oregano, minced
3	garlic cloves minced
1	teaspoon freshly ground black pepper

Season goose breasts with first 3 ingredients. In a non-metallic bowl, combine wine, oil and vinegar. Add goose breasts, cover and refrigerate for 4 to 6 hours. Drain and reserve marinade. Cook goose breasts on a medium barbecue until rare. Meanwhile, heat reserved marinade in a small pan until hot. Place cooked goose breasts in a plastic container with a tight-fitting lid. Add remaining ingredients and heated marinade. Place lid on container securely, shake up container to mix ingredients and allow to stand for 10 minutes without removing lid. Return goose to barbecue for additional heat, if needed. Slice goose breasts across the "grain," arrange on a platter and spoon herbs over sliced meat.

THAI-SPICED
PINTAIL BREASTS

Increase amount of red curry paste for a fiery version of this dish.

6 servings

8-10	pintail breast halves
2	tablespoons honey
1	tablespoon red curry paste
½	teaspoon turmeric
¼	teaspoon ground cinnamon
1	tablespoon fresh ginger,
	peeled and minced
½	cup soy sauce
2	tablespoons peanut oil
1	tablespoon sugar
2	tablespoons rice vinegar
1	garlic clove, minced
½	cup water
	salt and pepper to taste

In a small bowl, combine honey, curry paste, turmeric, cinnamon, ginger and half of the soy sauce. Brush mixture over duck breasts, place into a container with any leftover marinade, cover and refrigerate for 15 to 24 hours.

Remove duck breasts, save marinade. In a heavy, large skillet over medium-high heat, heat oil and brown breasts on both sides, about 3 minutes each side. Add sugar, rice vinegar, garlic, water, remainder of soy sauce and reserved marinade. Cook for 2 to 3 minutes, remove duck breasts and bring to boil. Season with salt and pepper, as desired. Cut the duck into thin slices, arrange on each plate and spoon sauce evenly over each.

UPLAND GAME

Since growing up in Virginia with an abundance of bobwhite quail, wild turkey, mourning doves, ruffed grouse, squirrels and cottontail rabbits, I have always thoroughly enjoyed hunting all types of upland game. Few experiences can compare to the exhilaration of hunting behind a brace of well-trained pointing dogs on a crisp fall morning. From Gambel's quail found in Arizona, to western Idaho's Hungarian partridge and northern California's riceland pheasants, chasing upland birds is the impetus for my fondest hunting memories.

Reaping the rewards of a game bird hunt requires attention during preparation. Upland bird flavors are typically subtle and hardly "gamy." Very little, if any, marinating is called for. Cooking times are minimal. Of course, you can prepare a quail or grouse dish that "falls right off the bone" by stewing for several hours, but the finished product will taste more like the other ingredients than the bird itself. Tender, juicy game birds that taste like game birds should be cooked quickly with relatively high heat after judicious seasoning.

Light-fleshed game birds such as quail, chukar and pheasant should be just pink when cooked. Darker meat birds like doves and Hungarian partridge should be cooked in a similar fashion until firm, but juicy. With few exceptions, the skin should not be removed from the birds to protect the lean meat from drying out. If you do not like the taste of game bird skin, remove the skin after cooking. If desired cover the breasts with bacon, julienned vegetables or fresh herbs for additional protection and flavoring, especially if the skin has been removed or torn during cleaning. When cooked, the juice in the fattiest part of the thigh will run clear when pricked.

Practically any dish that calls for chicken can be substituted with rabbit or hare. I recommend that you experiment with your favorite chicken recipe. Don't tell your guests about the substitution until the meal is well under way. The tender beige flesh when cooked, is tougher and stringier in older animals than younger ones. Unless you are a collector of mounted large rabbits, avoid taking them if you have a chance of finding smaller rabbits.

It is universally recommended that you wear rubber gloves when cleaning rabbits to avoid exposure to the bacteria, tularemia, which causes flu-like symptoms in exposed humans. The disease can be transmitted by exposure to the skin and through eating an infected rabbit. It is also wise to cook rabbits thoroughly as the disease cannot be killed by freezing.

The following recipes can be adapted for use with all fowl, wild and domestic. Trim excess fat from commercially-raised chickens and game hens to more closely approximate the finished game dish.

Photo at left is from the recipe on page 36.
Pheasant Breast Napoleon with Roasted Garlic Vinaigrette.

BARBECUED DOVES
WITH PLUM SAUCE

Barbecuing doves beyond medium-rare can result in a tough, dry bird. For best results, heat up the barbecue and cook 'em fast and hot.

4 servings

	Plum Sauce (page 89)
16-20	whole mourning or white winged doves, skin intact
1	cup soy sauce
1	cup water
1	teaspoon ground ginger
½	cup brown sugar
½	cup rice vinegar

Combine last 5 ingredients in a large bowl. Add doves and marinate covered for 24 hours in refrigerator. Barbecue over medium-hot coals, turning to brown evenly on all sides. Total cooking time should not exceed 6 to 7 minutes. Arrange on plate and baste with plum sauce and serve with additional sauce for dipping.

BRAISED COTTONTAIL RABBIT
IN RED WINE WITH MUSHROOMS

Rabbit hunters love this tender small game animal when prepared properly.

6 servings

3	rabbits, cleaned and cut into 6 pieces (2 legs, 2 shoulders with front legs and 2 trimmed rib cage with fillets)
1	cup onions, coarsely chopped
⅔	cup carrots, diced into 1/4" cubes
½	cup red bell pepper, coarsely chopped
2	cups fresh mushrooms, halved
1	cup tomatoes, coarsely chopped
2	tablespoons garlic, minced
4	cups game bird stock or chicken broth
2	cups dry red wine
¼	cup olive oil
2	teaspoons fresh oregano, finely chopped
2	tablespoons fresh rosemary, finely chopped
2	tablespoons fresh basil, coarsely chopped
1	cup flour seasoned with salt and pepper
	salt and freshly ground pepper to taste

Pre-heat oven to 325° F. Place rabbit pieces in a sturdy paper or plastic bag. Add seasoned flour and shake to coat evenly. In a large sauce pan or stock pot, heat olive oil over medium high heat and brown rabbit pieces on all sides. Remove rabbit and set aside.

Add onions, carrots and peppers in pan and sauté until onions turn light brown. Add garlic, tomatoes, oregano and 1 T fresh rosemary. Add wine and stir to deglaze pan.

Reduce by one-half of original volume of liquid. Add chicken stock and rabbit. Place in pre-heated oven for 1 hour. Add mushrooms and remaining rosemary. Cook for 5 minutes more. Remove rabbit and mushrooms, arrange on serving dish and place in oven (turned off) to keep warm. Place sauce pan on stove over high heat and reduce liquid by three fourths or until liquid thickens. (Note: You can save some cooking time, if desired, by thickening sauce with a equal mixture of cornstarch and cold water, adding a little at a time until thickened) Season with salt and pepper. Once sauce is thickened, add basil and reduce heat. Remove warmed rabbit pieces and mushrooms from oven and pour sauce over each.

GAME BIRD PIE

A great dish for a busy week. Prepare a day or two ahead and heat to serve at dinner time.

4 - 6 servings

- 12 ounces basic pastry dough
- 1 pound cooked game bird meat, cut into small pieces
- ¼ cup butter
- 1 cup fresh mushrooms, sliced
- ½ cup flour
- ¼ teaspoon freshly ground black pepper
- 2 tablespoons fresh parsley, minced
  pinch salt
- ⅔ cup milk
- ⅓ cup game bird stock or chicken broth
- ⅓ cup gruyére or Swiss cheese, grated
- 1 egg

On a floured surface, divide pastry dough into 2 pieces and roll each into 2 — 11 inch circles. Cover with a damp towel and set aside. In a large sauce pan over medium heat, add 1/2 of the butter and sauté mushrooms for 3 minutes. Remove mushrooms. Add remaining butter, heat to melt, stir in flour and cook for 2 to 3 minutes. Add pepper, parsley, salt, milk and stock. Bring to boil and cook until thickened. Remove from heat and stir in mushrooms and meat. Allow mixture to cool and stir in cheese.

Place one of the pastry circles into the bottom of a lightly greased pie plate, allowing a rim of pastry to fall over edges of pie plate. Spread filling evenly over pastry. Place remaining pastry over mixture and crimp edges together with bottom pastry. Beat egg lightly and brush top layer of pastry. Bake in a pre- heated 400° F oven for 30 minutes or until pastry is golden brown. Allow to cool for 5 minutes before serving.

HERB ROASTED WILD TURKEY
WITH CHERRY CHUTNEY

If fresh herbs are not available, substitute with half-quantities of dry herbs even though the finished dish will have a less aromatic flavor. The turkey must be cleaned and plucked carefully so that the skin is intact.

4 - 6 servings

- Cherry Chutney (see page 85)
- 1 large tom turkey, skin intact
- ½ cup fresh basil, chopped
- 1 tablespoon fresh rosemary, minced
- 2 tablespoons fresh tarragon, finely chopped
- 4 garlic cloves, minced
  salt and pepper
- 10 strips thick-sliced smoked bacon

Preheat oven to 350° F. Starting at the neck opening and working towards the small part of the breast, carefully maneuver fingers between the skin and breast of the turkey. Chop 4 of the bacon strips into small pieces. Combine fresh herbs, garlic and chopped bacon and spread evenly between the skin and breast. Sprinkle with salt and pepper and place remaining bacon strips over the breast. Place in oven and roast 10 minutes for each pound of turkey. Remove turkey from oven when internal temperature reaches 145° F. Let turkey set for 10 minutes. Carve and serve with chutney.

HUNGARIAN PARTRIDGE

I first hunted these beautiful and tasty game birds in the Hell's Canyon region of Idaho's Snake River. Consider yourself lucky if you live in an area inhabited by "Huns."

4 servings

8-12 Hungarian partridges, whole with
      skin intact
  2 tablespoons vegetable oil
  4 smoked bacon strips, diced fine
  2 medium green bell peppers,
      julienned
  1 medium onion, julienned
  1 cup canned tomatoes with juice
  1 teaspoon paprika
  1 pinch dried thyme
    salt & fresh ground black pepper

Season birds lightly with salt and pepper. Heat oil in a large skillet over medium flame, and add bacon. Cook until transparent, but not crisp. Increase heat to medium-high, add partridges and brown on all sides, about 5 minutes. Reduce heat to medium and add onions and peppers, cooking for 2 minutes. Add remaining ingredients, cover and cook for 5 minutes. Season with salt and pepper as desired.

PAN-FRIED PHEASANT BREASTS
WITH TARRAGON MUSTARD SAUCE
A crispy coating protects against drying out lean pheasant breasts.

4 servings

4 - 6 boneless pheasant breast halves, cut in half, with skin intact
  2 large eggs
  2 tablespoons dry cooking sherry
  ¼ cup green onions, diced fine
  ½ cup flour, seasoned with garlic salt and pepper
  ¾ cup seasoned bread crumbs
  2 tablespoons butter
  2 tablespoons vegetable oil
  ¼ cup dry white wine
  ¼ cup dijon mustard
  2 tablespoons fresh tarragon, chopped fine
  1 teaspoon sugar
  ½ cup heavy cream
    salt and white pepper to taste

Pound pheasant breast pieces between waxed paper sheets until 1/4 inch thick. In a small bowl, beat eggs with sherry. Add green onions to egg mixture. Dredge pheasant thoroughly in seasoned flour and dip in egg mixture. Coat with bread crumbs, pressing crumbs into breast. Place on waxed paper and refrigerate for 2 to 3 hours.

In a large skillet, heat oil and butter over medium-high heat and pan-fry breast pieces until lightly browned, about 3 minutes per side. Remove, place on paper towels and keep warm. Deglaze skillet with wine for 2 minutes while loosening solids from pan with a wooden spoon or spatula. Add mustard, tarragon, sugar and cream. Cook until sauce thickens. Adjust seasoning with salt and pepper. Place two breast pieces per person on plate and spoon sauce over each.

JAMAICAN BARBECUED PHEASANT

This toned-down version of Jamaican "jerk" marinade will not over-power the delicate meat of the pheasant, but will certainly add a touch of fire to the finished dish.

4 servings

- 2 pheasants, skin intact and split into 4 halves
- ¾ cup soy sauce
- ½ cup red wine vinegar
- ¼ cup vegetable oil
- ¼ cup honey
- ½ cup green onions, including tops, diced
- 1 medium red onion, diced
- 1 jalapeño pepper, seeded and diced
- ½ teaspoon ground cloves
- ½ teaspoon ground nutmeg
- ½ teaspoon ground allspice
- ½ teaspoon chili flakes
- ¼ teaspoon freshly ground black pepper

Make an incision at the inside of the thigh and leg joints of each pheasant half, cutting through the skin to the joint. Rinse pheasant halves under cold water and pat dry with paper towels. Place remaining ingredients in a food processor or blender and blend for 15 to 20 seconds. Pour mixture over pheasant, coating evenly. Cover and refrigerate for 12 hours, turning occasionally to marinate.

When barbecue coals are ash white, move coals to the sides of the barbecue. Place pheasant halves, breast side down, in the center of the well-greased barbecue. If using a gas barbecue, heat to medium before adding pheasants to grill. Cook for 4 to 5 minutes, turning a quarter turn during cooking to create "diamond" grill marks on breasts. Flip pheasant halves over, cover and cook for 3 to 4 more minutes. Cooked meat should be barely pink at the breast bone.

PHEASANT
WITH CASHEWS AND SNOW PEAS

Incredible flavor and texture combines with moist pheasant breast pieces. Keep an eye on the clock. Cooking time shouldn't exceed six minutes.

4 servings

- 4 pheasant breast halves, skin removed and cut into 1 inch pieces
- 3 garlic cloves, minced
- 1 tablespoon dry cooking sherry
- 1 tablespoon soy sauce
- 3 tablespoons cornstarch
- 1 tablespoon hoisin sauce
- 2 tablespoons peanut oil
- ½ cup game bird stock or chicken broth
- 1 ½ cups snow peas, fresh or frozen, strings and ends removed
- ½ cup sliced water chestnuts
- ⅓ cup salted cashews

In a medium bowl thoroughly mix garlic, sherry, soy sauce, cornstarch and hoisin sauce. Add pheasant pieces. Cover and refrigerate for 30 minutes. Heat oil in a wok or large skillet over high heat. Add pheasant and marinade and stir-fry for 2 to 3 minutes or until meat is just firm. Stir in stock and cook for 2 minutes. Add snow peas and water chestnuts and cook for 1 minute. Stir in cashews and serve immediately.

PHEASANT BREAST NAPOLEON
WITH ROASTED GARLIC VINAIGRETTE

This colorful dish can be served as an entrée or in a scaled-down version as an appetizer. Save this one for special occasions when you really want to impress your guests. Napoleons can be assembled during the day, refrigerated and heated for service later in the evening.

4 servings

4	pheasant breast halves, skin removed
½	cup flour, seasoned with 1 teaspoon garlic salt and 1/2 teaspoon black pepper
2	eggs, lightly beaten with 1 tablespoon cold water
1½	cups seasoned bread crumbs
½	cup peanut or corn oil
8	slices eggplant, approximately 1/4 inch thick and 4 inches in diameter
2	tablespoons butter
1	cup pitted black olives, finely chopped

1	garlic clove, minced
1	teaspoon capers, mashed
2	teaspoons olive oil
2	anchovy fillets, or 1 tablespoon anchovy paste
1	bunch fresh basil
4	ounces goat cheese, softened (or substitute cream cheese)
½	cup sundried tomato pesto (see page 90)
1	cup tomatoes, seeded and diced
	freshly ground black pepper

Prepare vinaigrette (next page) and let stand at room temperature for 1 hour before serving. If vinaigrette separates, briefly return to processor or blender before serving. Cut each pheasant breast in half widthwise. Place each piece between wax paper sheets and pound lightly with the flat side of a mallet until meat is 1/8 to 1/4 inch thick. Dredge each piece in seasoned flour, dip in beaten eggs and coat with bread crumbs. In a large skillet over medium-high heat, heat oil until hot and fry each piece until lightly browned. Remove breast pieces and drain on paper towels. Discard oil, wipe skillet and melt butter over medium- high heat. Sauté eggplant slices in butter for 1 minute each side. Remove and drain on paper towels. In a small bowl, combine olives, capers, olive oil and anchovies. Mix well, breaking up anchovy fillets. Prepare sundried tomato pesto.

In a baking pan or casserole dish, lay out 4 eggplant slices, about 1 inch apart. Spread a thin layer of goat cheese over eggplant. Spread 1 1/2 tablespoon of the olive mixture (*tapenade*) over goat cheese. Pick basil leaves and place 3 to 5 leaves, depending on size of leaves, over olive mixture. Place pheasant over basil leaves. Spread pesto thinly over pheasant. Repeat steps for second layer. Place pan or dish in a 300° F oven for 6 to 8 minutes or until warmed throughout. Remove Napoleons with a spatula and place one on each plate. Chop remaining basil leaves and combine with tomatoes and vinaigrette. In a small saucepan, warm vinaigrette. Do not boil or sauce may separate. Drizzle a little vinaigrette over each and spoon remaining vinaigrette on plate around Napoleon. Grind pepper over each. (See photo on page 30)

ROASTED GARLIC
VINAIGRETTE

2   tablespoons shallot, finely
        chopped (or substitute the
        white part of green onions)
⅓   cup white wine vinegar
1   tablespoon dijon mustard
½   teaspoon salt
1   pinch white pepper
1   egg, white only
4   garlic cloves, roasted in a 350° F
        oven until softened and
        lightly browned
1   cup olive oil

In a food processor or blender, process
first 7 ingredients until blended. While machine is running, add oil in a thin stream
until emulsified.

*Note: If you do not have a processor or
blender, mash the garlic in a medium bowl,
add other ingredients except oil and whisk
in oil, a little at a time until emulsified.*

STUFFED PHEASANT BREAST
MEDALLIONS

For best results, you'll need a very sharp boning knife.

4 servings

4   pheasant breast halves, skin intact
4   slices Canadian bacon
1   large red bell pepper, roasted, peeled,
        seeded and cut into 4 sections
12   fresh basil leaves
4   garlic cloves, roasted and mashed into paste
2   tablespoons olive oil
¼   teaspoons salt
½   teaspoons freshly ground black pepper

Preheat oven to 425° F. Place the pheasant breast halves on a cutting surface and cut a "pocket"
into each by inserting a sharp boning knife into the side of the breast and making a cut as wide as
a slice of Canadian bacon. Work the knife throughout the breast carefully. Do not puncture the
flesh other than at the entrance point.

On each slice of Canadian bacon, spread an equal amount of the roasted garlic paste, top with a
section of red pepper and 3 basil leaves. Carefully, fold the Canadian bacon and insert into
pheasant pocket. Fold the edges of the breast down to cover the pocket opening, working the skin
down evenly to cover the top of the stuffed breast. Place each breast side-by-side in a small baking
pan as snugly as possible. Brush breasts with olive oil and season with salt and pepper.

Place in oven and bake until browned, about 10 to 12 minutes. Remove from oven. Allow to cool
slightly and slice each breast with the boning knife into 2 or 3 medallions. Arrange on plate.

CRISPY BAKED
PHEASANT

An alternative to deep-frying, crunchy pheasant pieces with plenty of character. Try it with sweet summer corn on the cob, coleslaw and a glass of freshly brewed iced tea.

4 servings

2   pheasants, skin intact, cut into 6 pieces each (breast, leg, thigh)
1   cup flour seasoned with 1 tablespoon garlic powder, 1 tablespoon onion powder and 1 tablespoon dried basil flakes
3   eggs, lightly beaten with 3 table-spoons dijon mustard
2   cups seasoned bread crumbs
1   tablespoon cracked black popper
3   tablespoons mustard seeds
3   tablespoons sesame seeds
2   tablespoons celery seeds
½   teaspoon salt

Dredge pheasant pieces in seasoned flour to coat evenly. Coat each floured piece with egg mixture. Combine remaining ingredients in a medium bowl and mix well. Roll each pheasant piece in coating mixture and refrigerate for 30 minutes. Pre-heat oven to 375° F. Bake pheasant pieces in a lightly greased baking dish, uncovered, until golden brown, about 35 to 40 minutes.

RABBIT FLORENTINE

Subtle seasonings complement the delightful, moist rabbit pieces.

4 servings

1 ½   cups rabbit, boned and cut into 1 inch pieces
½   cup flour
1   teaspoon garlic salt
1   teaspoon onion powder
½   teaspoon freshly ground black pepper
½   teaspoon ground nutmeg
4   strips smoked bacon, diced
3   tablespoons olive oil
2   garlic cloves, minced
½   cup yellow onion, diced
⅔   cup game stock or beef broth
1   cup fresh mushrooms, sliced thin
8   ounces spinach leaves, washed and stalks removed
salt and pepper to taste
⅓   cup goat cheese, crumbled (optional)
4   cups cooked white rice

In a paper bag, combine flour, garlic salt, onion powder, pepper and nutmeg. Place rabbit pieces in bag and coat evenly with flour mixture. In a large skillet over medium heat, cook bacon until browned. Remove bacon and set aside. Heat oil and brown rabbit pieces evenly on all sides. Add garlic and onion and cook for 3 minutes. Stir in game stock, bring to boil, cover and cook for 5 minutes. Remove cover, add mushrooms and cook for 2 minutes. Add spinach leaves and stir until spinach is just-cooked. Season with salt and pepper. Remove from heat. Place one cup of warm cooked rice on each plate. Ladle rabbit and sauce equally over each and top with goat cheese and cooked bacon.

RABBIT JAMBALAYA

If you don't have three rabbits lying around, substitute them with, or add ducks or game birds to this traditional Cajun dish to yield 6 cups of cubed meat.

6 - 8 servings

8   ounces andouille sausage, cut into 1/4 inch slices (you may substitute other spicy, smoked pure-pork sausage)
2   tablespoons butter
2   tablespoons vegetable oil
⅓   cup flour, seasoned with 1 teaspoon *each* salt, garlic powder, onion powder, black pepper and paprika
3   cottontail rabbits, boned and cut into 1/2 inch cubes
1   medium yellow onion, diced
1   green bell pepper, diced
2   celery stalks, diced
3   garlic cloves, minced
1   tablespoon brown sugar
2   teaspoons paprika
2   bay leaves

1   teaspoon dried basil leaves
¾   teaspoon dried thyme leaves
¾   teaspoon cayenne pepper
½   teaspoon black pepper
½   teaspoon garlic powder
    dash Tabasco
1   14 ½ oz can diced tomatoes, not drained
1   cup tomato sauce
3   cups game bird stock or chicken broth
2   cups uncooked white rice
1   cup green onions, tops included, diced
½   cup fresh parsley, minced

In a paper bag, add seasoned flour and rabbit pieces. Toss to coat meat lightly. In a large heavy stock pot over medium-high heat, add half of the oil and butter. Cook sausage for 2 to 3 minutes. Add rabbit and cook until lightly browned. Remove rabbit and sausage from pot and add remaining oil and butter, cooking over medium-high heat. Add onion, bell pepper, celery and garlic. Cook for 3 minutes. Stir in brown sugar and cook for 2 more minutes. Add remaining ingredients except rice, green onions and parsley. Bring to a boil, reduce heat to low and simmer for 25 minutes. Add rabbit and sausage and cook for 10 to 15 minutes. Stir in rice, bring back to boil. Reduce heat to low, cover and simmer for 25 minutes. Stir in green onions and parsley and remove from heat. Adjust seasoning with salt and pepper. Serve in large bowls.

ROASTED QUAIL
WITH RED BELL PEPPER SAUCE

Fortunately, quail season coincides with late-season red bell peppers which can be a bit pricey in the winter and spring Serve with Two-Color Polenta (see page 80).

4 servings

8   quail with skin intact
3   garlic cloves, minced
1   tablespoon lemon pepper
4   slices smoked bacon, cut in half
1   cup Grilled Red Bell Pepper Sauce
    (see page 87)

Rub quail with garlic, season with lemon pepper and place 2 bacon halves over each breast. Place breast side up in a roasting pan and roast in a pre-heated 475° F oven for 8 to 10 minutes. Since oven temperatures vary greatly, be careful not to overcook birds. Check occasionally to make certain that quail is still tender and not overcooked. Cooked breast meat should be barely pink when done. Remove quail from oven, place 2 on each plate and drizzle sauce over each.

RABBIT
WITH PENNE PASTA AND ANCHOVY SAUCE

When it comes to anchovies, most people either like them or they don't. If you fall into the first group, you'll love this simple rabbit dish.

4 servings

1   rabbit, boned and cut into small pieces
2   tablespoons olive oil
8   anchovy fillets
¼   teaspoon freshly ground black pepper
2   garlic, minced
½   cup parma ham, diced (or substitute just-cooked diced smoked bacon)
¼   cup dry red wine
2   cups tomato sauce
1   cup fresh tomato, diced
3   tablespoons fresh parsley, chopped
¼   cup black olives, sliced
4   cups cooked penne pasta
2   tablespoons butter
¼   cup Parmesan cheese, grated

Heat oil and brown rabbit pieces lightly in a large skillet over medium-high heat. Add anchovies, garlic and pepper. Cook for 3 to 4 minutes, stirring 2 or 3 times. Add ham or bacon and cook for 3 minutes. Add wine and cook for 2 minutes. Add tomato sauce, bring to boil, reduce heat to low, cover and cook for 6 to 8 minutes. Add diced tomato, parsley and black olives. Cook for 3 minutes more. Toss warm pasta with butter. Top with sauce and sprinkle Parmesan cheese over sauce.

SAUTEED QUAIL
WITH APPLE CREAM SAUCE

The delicate flavor of quail is enhanced by this flavorful sauce

4 servings

- 12 quail, skin intact
- ⅛ teaspoon white pepper
- ⅛ teaspoon salt
- ⅛ teaspoon ground coriander
- 2 tablespoons butter
- ¾ cup dry white wine juice of 1/2 lemon
- 1 tablespoon shallot, minced
- 1 firm Granny Smith apple, peeled and diced very fine
- 1 tablespoon honey
- ½ cup heavy cream
  salt and white pepper to taste

Season quail lightly with pepper, salt and coriander. In a large skillet over medium heat, melt butter and lightly brown quail on all sides about 2 to 3 minutes per side. Remove quail, increase heat to medium-high and de-glaze pan with 2 tablespoons of the wine, scraping pan to remove solids. Add remaining wine, lemon juice and shallots and reduce liquid by one-half. Add apple, honey and cream and return quail to pan. Reduce until liquid thickens. Season with salt and pepper to taste. Place 3 quail per person on plate and spoon sauce evenly over each.

QUAIL
WITH ORANGE-HONEY GLAZE

A great quick and easy recipe

4 servings

- 8 quail, skin intact
- ½ teaspoon powdered coriander
- 5 tablespoons unsalted butter
- 1 tablespoon olive oil
- 2 tablespoons honey
- ¼ cup freshly squeezed
    orange juice
  salt and freshly ground pepper

Rinse quail and pat dry with paper towels. Season lightly with salt, pepper and coriander.

In a large skillet over medium-high heat, combine 2 tablespoons butter, olive oil and 1 tablespoon honey. Add the quail and sauté for about 5 to 6 minutes or until quail is lightly browned on all sides. Add remaining honey and orange juice and cook until liquid starts to thicken. Remove quail and arrange on plate. Remove skillet from heat and whisk in remaining butter. Season as desired with salt and pepper. Pour sauce over each quail.

BIG GAME

Among game-shy individuals, big game animals frequently receive the unwarranted distinction of being unpleasant tasting. While mature males taken during rutting season may be a bit tougher and more pronounced in flavor than a young animal, the most important influences on the quality of the finished dish are the handling of the animal immediately after the hunt and the method of transportation and storage. To guarantee the most flavorful finished product, all large game animals should be carefully field-dressed, butchered, labeled and refrigerated or frozen as soon as possible.

You may choose to marinate antlered game prior to cooking. My favorite marinade consists of a hearty dry red wine, garlic, pickling spices and a touch of a good vinegar. Be careful not to marinade more than 24 hours since the meat may actually get tougher with prolonged marinating. Some meats, like bear, will benefit from marinating, particularly if your guests include neophyte wild game diners. Vacuum packaging is a good way to marinate quickly. The process opens the pores of the meats and vegetables, allowing better and faster penetration of the marinade. Normal marinating times of two to eight hours can be reduced to 15 to 30 minutes when vacuum packaged with FoodSaver.

It is wise to invest in a good meat thermometer to determine the doneness of large game. Experience will allow you to rely on finger pressure to test for the temperature of the cooked meat. The less the meat gives to pressure, the more it is cooked. Periodically place a firm finger or two on the meat during cooking. You'll discover that the period of time required for the meat to turn from medium-rare to beyond redemption is remarkably brief. Avoid making test cuts into the meat while it cooks, unless that is part of an anticipated ritual among you and your guests. Searing the outside of game meats will help to seal in flavor and moisture. Sampling during cooking with an occasional cut, will not.

Beyond medium-rare, antlered game will quickly toughen. If your guests usually cringe at the sight of rare meat, carve the meat out of sight and cover it with a rich, ruby red wine sauce. Temperatures should range from 130°F (rare) to 145°F (medium-rare). All bear and wild pigs should be cooked to at least 150°F as a precaution against trichinosis.

While the recipes within this section specify a particular type of big game animal, all are interchangeable. Deer, elk and caribou can be used for any dish specifying one of these animals. I prefer to marinate stronger tasting antelope. Bear roasts work well with either the Herb Crust (page 47, found within the Herb-Crusted Elk Leg Roast recipe), or the Fruity Crust (page 50, found within the Wild Boar Roast recipe).

Photo at left is from the recipe on page 47.
Brandy-Peppercorn Venison Steak

Wild boar recipes work equally well with trimmed pork. All antlered game recipes can be used with similar cuts of beef.

BBQ'D CARIBOU STEAK
WITH BLEU CHEESE
AND GRILLED ONIONS

Easy preparation of my favorite big game animal

4 servings

- 4   6 - 8 ounce caribou sirloin steaks
- ½   teaspoon garlic powder
- ½   teaspoon onion powder
- ½   teaspoon freshly ground black pepper
- 1   pinch salt
- ¼   cup Worcestershire sauce
- 2   tablespoons sugar
- 4   large whole onion slices, intact
- ⅓   cup bleu cheese crumbles

Combine garlic powder, onion powder, black pepper and salt and sprinkle over steaks. Cover and refrigerate for 1 hour. In a small bowl, mix Worcestershire sauce and sugar and immerse onion slices to coat thoroughly.

Place steaks and onion slices on a well-greased medium-hot charbroiler or barbecue kettle. Cook steaks approximately 3 minutes per side or until meat is rare to medium-rare. Cook onion slices until just soft and lightly browned on both sides, turning carefully with a spatula.

Place onion slice on each steak and top with equal portion of crumbled bleu cheese.

BAKED BOAR RIBS
WITH SWEET-HOT BARBECUE SAUCE

It takes a few of these lean ribs to make a meal. Prolonged baking in sauce will make the meat fall right off the bone

4 servings

- 6-8 pounds boar ribs, sawed in half, if possible
       black pepper
       garlic powder
- 3   cups Sweet-Hot Barbecue Sauce (see page 88)

Baking Sauce

- 12   ounces flat beer
- 2   lemons, sliced into fourths
- 1   large yellow onion, sliced into rings
- ½   cup cider vinegar
- 3   garlic cloves, minced
- ½   cup brown sugar
- 2   cups tomato sauce
- 2   tablespoons tomato paste
- ¼   cup soy sauce
- ¼   cup Worcestershire sauce
- ½   teaspoon black pepper
- ½   teaspoon cayenne pepper

Combine above ingredients in a large sauce pan or stock pot and bring to a boil. Reduce heat and cook for 5 minutes.

Liberally season ribs with black pepper and garlic powder. Arrange in a large roasting pan and place in a 450° F oven until well browned on both sides, about 6 to 8 minutes per side. Pour baking sauce over ribs, cover, lower heat to 375° F and bake for 1 1/2 to 2 hours, turning frequently to bake ribs evenly. Remove ribs from oven when meat can be pulled free from the bone. Pour off baking sauce and discard. Brush ribs with barbecue sauce and return to oven for 10 minutes more. Serve with additional sauce on the side.

BOAR
WITH BLACK BEAN SAUCE

My favorite wild boar recipe
Prepare ahead and warm before serving

6 servings

¾ cup cooked black beans, rinsed and
    smashed into paste
⅔ cup dry sherry
⅓ cup soy sauce
4 garlic cloves, minced
2 teaspoons fresh ginger, minced
1 tablespoon brown sugar
3 tablespoons rice vinegar
½ teaspoon sesame oil
2 ½ pounds boar stew meat, sinew removed
    and cut into 1 inch cubes
3 tablespoons peanut oil
1 cup game stock or beef broth
1 medium yellow onion, coarse chopped
1 large red bell pepper, coarse chopped
2 tablespoons cornstarch mixed with
2 tablespoons cold water
    freshly ground black pepper to taste

Combine black beans, sherry, soy sauce, garlic, ginger, sugar, vinegar and sesame oil. Add boar meat, toss, cover and refrigerate for 1 hour. In a wok or large heavy duty skillet over medium-high heat, heat oil. Remove meat from sauce, reserve sauce and brown meat evenly in oil. Add sauce and game stock and bring to boil. Reduce heat to low, cover and simmer, stirring occasionally, for 45 minutes to 1 hour or until boar meat softens and pieces can be broken apart easily with your fingers. Add onion and bell pepper, increase heat to medium and cook 3 to 4 minutes or until onions become translucent. Stir in cornstarch mixture, a little at a time, until sauce thickens. Season with pepper.

BLACKENED ELK STEAK

You'll need a cast iron skillet,
an oxygen tank and a taste for Cajun spice

4 servings

4 10 ounce elk sirloin or top round steaks,
    cut as thick as possible
2 tablespoons peanut oil
1 teaspoon garlic powder
1 teaspoon onion powder
½ teaspoon dried thyme
½ teaspoon cayenne pepper
½ teaspoon black pepper
½ teaspoon white pepper
1 tablespoon paprika
½ cup sour cream

Rub or brush steaks with oil. Combine remaining ingredients and coat steaks evenly with spice mixture. Heat a large cast iron skillet over high heat in a well-ventilated area. The skillet must be "white hot."

Note: Restaurants featuring blackened meats and fish will leave the skillet on over high heat throughout meal periods. The blackening process can be a smoky one. Blackening without substantial heat will result in a more oily steak and the time required to blacken the meat will cause the meat to be overcooked and dry. Open the windows and let your neighbors know that there's no need to call the fire department. Also, try not to breathe in the fumes since they can irritate your respiratory system. Are you sure you want to try this? You bet!

Place steaks in the skillet for about 3 minutes per side until blackened, but not cooked beyond medium-rare. Carefully remove steaks from skillet and place 2 tablespoons of sour cream over each.

WILD BOAR CHILE VERDE

Serve with warm flour tortillas and cold Mexican beer

6 - 8 servings

- 3 pounds boar shoulder, cut into 1 inch pieces
- 3 tablespoons olive oil
- 2 cups yellow onion, chopped
- 8 garlic cloves, chopped
- 1 cup green bell pepper, chopped
- 1 cup red bell pepper, chopped
- 1 cup Anaheim pepper, chopped
- 3 jalapeño peppers, seeds removed and diced fine
- 1 tablespoon dried oregano flakes
- 2 tablespoons chili powder
- 2 tablespoons cumin
- 1 teaspoon cayenne pepper
- 2 cups fresh tomatillos, quartered
    (or canned, juice removed)
- 4-5 cups chicken broth
- 1 cup fresh cilantro
    salt and pepper to taste

In a large stock pot, heat oil over medium-high flame. Add boar and lightly brown on all sides. Add onion, garlic and peppers and sauté until onion is translucent. Add oregano, chili powder, cumin, cayenne pepper, tomatillos and enough chicken broth to a level just below the top of the other ingredients. Lower heat and simmer 1 hour, adding more chicken broth as needed to keep mixture moist. Check meat to see if it has softened and begun to shred. If not, simmer for additional time. Add cilantro and simmer for 10 more minutes.

Caution: When preparing hot peppers such as jalapeños, make sure to wear rubber gloves and wash hands thoroughly afterwards. If you cut a jalapeño and then touch your eyes, you will appreciate this word of caution.

BRAISED ELK ROAST
WITH VEGETABLES AND HERBS

Sensational cold weather dish for hearty appetites

6 servings

- 2-3 pounds elk shoulder roast, trimmed of fat and silver skin, cut into six equal portions
- 6 smoked bacon slices, diced
- 3 tablespoons peanut oil
- 12 pearl onions
- 3 celery stalks, cut into 2 inch pieces
- 4 med. carrots, peeled and cut into 1 inch pieces
- 10 new red potatoes, halved
- 4 garlic cloves, sliced
- 1 ½ cups red wine
- ¾ cup game stock or beef broth
- 3 bay leaves
- 2 tablespoons fresh rosemary, diced fine
- 1 tablespoon fresh thyme, chopped
- 2 tablespoons fresh sage, chopped
- ½ teaspoon salt
- ½ teaspoon freshly ground pepper

In a heavy stock pot, heat oil over medium-high heat and brown bacon. Add elk and brown evenly on all sides. Add onion, celery, carrots, potatoes and carrots. Stir in and cook for 3-4 minutes. Add wine, stock and bay leaves. Cover, reduce heat to low and simmer for 2 hours. Add fresh herbs, salt and pepper and cook, covered, for 30 more minutes. Serve in large bowls with a fresh herb garnish and warm bread.

BRANDY-PEPPERCORN
VENISON STEAK

For a low-fat version of this dish, omit the heavy cream

4 servings

4   7 ounce venison steaks, trimmed
1   tablespoon soft green peppercorns
1   tablespoon pink peppercorns
1   tablespoon black pepper, coarse ground
2   tablespoons whole grain mustard
2   tablespoons olive or peanut oil
2   garlic cloves, minced
½   cup game stock or beef broth
¼   cup brandy
½   cup heavy cream
    salt to taste

Combine peppercorns and black pepper in a bowl and mash together with a spoon. Coat venison steaks with mustard and rub peppercorn mixture over steaks. Heat oil in a large skillet over medium-high. Add garlic and sauté for 2 minutes. Add steaks and brown on both sides, about 3 to 4 minutes each side. Pour all but 1 teaspoon of the brandy over steaks and cook for 2 minutes. *Caution: Brandy may ignite! Keep away from any flame until alcohol burns off*

Remove steaks from pan and keep warm. Add stock or broth, scraping pan with a spoon or spatula to loosen peppercorns, garlic and venison scraps and cook until liquid is reduced by one-half. Add cream and cook until sauce thickens. Place steaks on a plate and spoon equal quantities of sauce over each.

HERB - CRUSTED
ELK LEG ROAST

The herb crust adds remarkable flavor and seals in moisture

4 - 6 servings

1   2 ½ to 3 pound elk leg roast, boned, gristle
    and silver skin removed
1   cup dry red wine
2   tablespoons Worcestershire sauce
1   teaspoon coarse grind black pepper
¼   cup flour seasoned with salt and pepper
8   ounces butter, softened
2   tablespoons fresh rosemary, minced
2   tablespoons fresh sage, minced
1   tablespoon fresh thyme, minced
1   tablespoon fresh tarragon, minced
3   garlic cloves, minced
2   shallots, minced
¾   cup seasoned bread crumbs
1   teaspoon coarse ground black pepper

Combine wine, Worcestershire sauce and 1 teaspoon pepper for marinade. Marinate roast for 24 hours in refrigerator.

Pre heat oven to 450° F. Remove roast from marinade and pat dry. *Herb Crust:* Sift seasoned flour over roast. Combine remaining ingredients to make a paste. Place the roast in a roasting pan and spread the paste evenly over top and sides of roast, applying hand pressure to help paste adhere to roast. Place in oven for 10 minutes, reduce oven temperature to 375° F and cook until center of roast is 135° F to 140° F, about 25 more minutes. Remove from oven and let stand for 10 minutes before carving into equal portions.

STUFFED ELK ROAST
WITH SWEET AND SOUR ZINFANDEL SAUCE

Don't let the directions scare you. This preparation is easier than you
may think and you'll get better with practice.

6 servings

Sweet and Sour Zinfandel Sauce (see page 88)

1	2 ½ to 3 pound boneless elk shoulder roast
12	ounces peppered Monterey Jack cheese, grated
1	bunch fresh basil
6	ounces prosciutto, deli-shaved (have your butcher slice as thin as possible without shredding the prosciutto)

1	tablespoon fresh ground black pepper
3	garlic cloves, mashed into paste
	butcher string for tying roast
2	tablespoons olive oil

BUTTERFLYING YOUR ROAST

Trim any excess fat, gristle and silver skin from the roast. Be careful not to make any deep knife cuts into the roast while trimming so that the butterflied roast will remain intact. Lay the roast on a cutting surface and begin butterflying by making a knife cut through the bottom third of the roast along the side, stopping about 3/4 of an inch before slicing through the roast. Open the roast at the "hinge" and make a second cut through the larger section, starting at the hinge, stopping the cut again 3/4 inch before slicing through the roast, following the path of the first cut. Flatten the roast with the palm of your hand.

> *Note: For especially thick roasts, butterfly the meat into four or five "hinged" sections.*
> *Meat should be no more than 1/2 to 3/4 inches thick before stuffing.*

Pick whole basil leaves and lay flat on the butterflied roast, covering the entire inside surface. Distribute the grated cheese evenly over the basil. Lay the prosciutto in strips over the cheese. Cut a piece of string 3 feet long. Begin rolling roast by folding, grasping an edge parallel to the hinges and folding the first inch of the edge over tightly. Continue rolling the roast carefully, tucking in the stuffing as the roast is rolled. Use both hands to insure that the roast is rolled as snugly as possible. Loop the string over one end and make a knot. Continue looping the string around the roast and pull the long end of the string through each loop, pulling tightly each time, until you reach the end of the roast. Tie off the string and cut off any excess. Rub garlic over the roast and coat with pepper.

In an oven-safe skillet over medium-high flame, heat olive oil. Place the roast in the skillet and sear until it is browned on all sides. Place skillet in a 375°F oven for 12 to 15 minutes or until meat is cooked to medium-rare. Remove roast from oven and let it sit for 5 minutes. Remove string and slice into 6 sections. Spoon sauce on each plate and place roast section on sauce.

ELK TENDERLOIN
WITH CRISPY CORNMEAL CREPES AND FRESH PAPAYA

A combination of flavors, textures and presentation does justice to the choicest cut of antlered game

4 servings

2 pounds elk tenderloin, trimmed of fat and sinew
12 cornmeal crepes (see below)
1 cup sour cream
1 teaspoon freshly squeezed lemon juice
¼ teaspoon ground coriander
1 cup red bell pepper, finely diced

2 cups fresh papaya, peeled, seeded and diced into
  1/4 inch cubes
1 cup red bell pepper, finely diced
¼ cup fresh cilantro leaves, diced
1 tablespoon freshly squeezed lime juice
¼ teaspoon ground cumin
  salt and freshly ground black pepper

Prepare cornmeal crepes as directed. Season tenderloin with salt and black pepper. Combine sour cream, lemon juice and coriander. Mix well to blend. In a separate bowl, toss papaya with remaining ingredients. Roast tenderloin in a 425° F oven until internal temperature is 135°F, about 8 to 12 minutes, depending on the thickness of the meat. Remove from oven and let stand for 3 to 4 minutes. Cut meat into 4 equal portions and slice each portion into 5 slices. Return to oven for a minute or two, if necessary, to warm meat. Fan 3 crepes across two-thirds of each plate, placing towards one side of the plates and leaving one-third of the plate uncovered. Place one-fourth of the sour cream mixture on the center of the plate, on the inside edges of the fanned crepes. Mound one-fourth of the papaya mixture on the center of the sour cream. Fan the tenderloin slices, overlapping the edges of each slice, against the papaya and towards the uncovered portion of the plates.

CORNMEAL CREPES

¾ cup flour
¼ cup yellow cornmeal
1 medium egg
1 pinch salt

2 tablespoons butter, melted
1 cup water
2 tablespoons beer

In a medium bowl, combine flour and cornmeal. Add egg and salt and mix in. Mix in 1 tablespoon of the butter, a little at a time. Slowly mix in water and beat batter until creamy. Cover and refrigerate for 3 hours. Remove from refrigerator and stir in beer. Heat a crepe pan or small non-stick pan over medium-high heat and add remaining 1 tablespoon of butter. Wipe pan with towel. Ladle a small amount of batter onto center of pan, moving pan quickly to coat bottom with a very thin layer of batter. Cook until lightly browned, flip crepe and cook other side. If crepes do not crisp, place side by side on a baking sheet in a 400° F oven for 4 to 5 minutes.

WILD BOAR ROAST
WITH A FRUITY CRUST

*The aroma of this savory roast is surpassed
only by its magnificent flavor.*

6 - 8 servings

- 1   3 to 4 pound boneless wild boar loin, trimmed
- 2   eggs
- 1   cup flour
- ¾   cup seasoned bread crumbs
- 2   tablespoons fresh rosemary, minced
- 3   garlic cloves, minced
- 1   teaspoon freshly ground black pepper
- ½   teaspoon salt
- ¼   teaspoon ground nutmeg
- 2   tablespoons honey
- 2   tablespoons grated orange peel
- 1   tablespoon grated lemon peel
- ½   cup fresh (preferably) or canned pineapple, mashed into paste
- 1   Granny Smith apple, peeled and grated

Completely dust roast with 1/4 cup of the flour. *Fruity Crust:* In a bowl, combine remaining ingredients and mix well into paste. Spread paste evenly over bottom of roast and place in a roasting pan. Spread remaining paste over top and sides of roast. Place in a 450° F oven for 10 minutes to lightly brown the crust. Reduce heat to 350° F, cover and roast for 25 to 30 minutes more or until internal temperature reaches 155° F. Remove from oven, let stand for 5 minutes and slice with a sharp, thin knife into 1/4 to 1/2 inch thick slices. Try to keep crust as intact as possible while slicing.

STUFFED BOAR CHOPS
WITH PORT WINE SAUCE

*Great with garlic mashed potatoes and a glass
of peppery zinfandel.*

4 servings

Port Wine Sauce (see page 89)

- 4   1 ½ to 2 inch-thick chops
- 2   tablespoons vegetable oil
- 4   ounces cream cheese, softened
- ⅓   cup walnut pieces
- ½   cup dried apricots, diced
- 1   tablespoon shallot or green onion, minced
- 1   tablespoon fresh rosemary, minced
- 1   tablespoon fresh thyme
  salt and freshly ground black pepper

With a sharp boning knife, cut a 2 inch slit into the side of each chop. Work the knife into the chop, forming a "pocket" for the stuffing. Season each chop with salt and pepper. Combine the remaining ingredients and stuff equal amounts into each pocket.

In an oven-safe skillet over medium heat, brown chops lightly. Place in pre-heated 375° F oven until meat is firm and stuffing begins to run out, about 20 to 25 minutes. Top each chop with port wine sauce.

EAST/WEST
VENISON MEDALLIONS

Asian and Western flavors team up to create this quick and delicious venison dish. Prepare ingredients ahead and stir-fry just before serving while your guests take in the magnificent aroma.

4 servings

1 ½	pounds boneless venison leg or shoulder roast, trimmed of silver skin and sinew
¼	cup low-sodium soy sauce
½	teaspoon sesame oil
½	cup dry red wine
3	tablespoons rice vinegar
1	teaspoon dried oregano
½	teaspoon dried thyme
¼	teaspoon chili powder
2	tablespoons molasses
1	tablespoon peanut oil
2	garlic cloves, minced
¼	medium red onion, coarsely chopped
½	medium red bell pepper coarsely chopped
¼	cup fresh basil, chopped
1	cup Chinese pea pods, ends and strings removed
¼	cup sliced water chestnuts
1	tablespoon cornstarch mixed with equal part cold water
	freshly ground black pepper to taste

Cut venison into 12 equal pieces. With the flat side of a mallet, lightly pound each piece into round medallions of approximately equal thickness. Combine next 8 ingredients and marinate medallions, covered, for 2 hours in refrigerator. Heat oil in a medium-high wok or large skillet and add garlic. Cook for 1 minute. Remove medallions from marinade and stir-fry for 2 minutes. Add onions and peppers and stir-fry for 2 minutes more. Add marinade and bring to boil. Add remaining ingredients and stir-fry until sauce thickens, about 2 to 3 minutes. Season with pepper and serve.

CHARLES SPINETTA'S
VENISON ROAST

The Charles Spinetta Winery and Gallery in Plymouth, California, has done a great deal to support sportsmen's groups including Ducks Unlimited, Quail Unlimited and California Waterfowl Association. If you are in the area, stop by and have a glass of wine with Charlie and browse through the winery's spectacular wildlife art gallery. Each of Spinetta's varietal wines features a beautiful label featuring renowned wildlife artists Joe Garcia and Sherrie Russell Meline. Charlie is a devoted outdoorsman and a great wild game chef as evidenced by the following recipe.

4 - 6 servings

2 - 3	pounds venison roast, fat and sinew removed and butterflied. (See Page 48)
1	cup Charles Spinetta Zinfandel
⅓	cup red wine vinegar
½	cup olive oil
1	red onion, diced
6	garlic cloves, minced
1	tablespoon juniper berries, crushed
1	tablespoon freshly ground black pepper
½	teaspoon salt
3	bay leaves

Prepare venison roast as specified. Combine remaining ingredients and whisk to blend well. Lay butterflied roast out flat in a shallow container. Pour marinade over meat, cover and refrigerate for 6 to 8 hours, turning meat over every 2 hours. Remove meat from marinade. Starting from the shortest edge, roll roast tightly and tie securely. Roast in a pre-heated 450° F degree oven for 5 minutes. Reduce heat to 375° F and roast for an additional 15 minutes or until internal temperature reaches 135° F to 140° F. Remove roast from oven, let stand for 2 to 3 minutes. Remove string and slice into equal portions. Serve with a glass of Charles Spinetta Zinfandel.

KOREAN BARBECUED
VENISON STEAK

This recipe is inspired by an innovative home chef, Jeanne Bernardi, and was intended to be used with beef flank steak. I think it works equally well with all antlered game, particularly those cuts which can be a bit tough.

4 servings

2   pounds venison cross rib (shoulder) roast, sinew
    removed and cut into 4 equal portions and then
    each portion cut into 3 equal pieces
⅓   cup soy sauce
3   tablespoons sesame oil
3   garlic cloves, minced
3   tablespoons sesame seeds
⅓   teaspoon black pepper
2   teaspoons fresh ginger, minced
    or ½ teaspoon ground ginger
⅔   cup green onions, diced fine
⅓   cup brown sugar
12 bamboo skewers,
    soaked for 30 minutes in water

On a firm surface or cutting board, pound venison pieces with the flat side of a mallet into ½ inch thick strips. Combine remaining ingredients in a bowl, add meat and toss. Cover and refrigerate for 24 hours. (For faster turnaround use your FoodSaver vacuum packaging system). Skewer marinated meat on bamboo skewers and grill over white-hot coals or medium-hot gas barbecue for 2 to 3 minutes per side or until medium-rare.

VENISON
WITH TOMATOES AND GREEN PEPPERS

*This popular Chinese beef dish tastes
even better with venison.*

4 servings

1   pound venison round steak, sliced into
    ¼ inch thick strips
½   teaspoon freshly ground black pepper
2   tablespoons peanut oil
2   garlic cloves, minced
½   teaspoon fresh ginger, minced
¼   cup soy sauce
½   teaspoon sugar
1   large green bell pepper, cut into 1 inch squares
2   medium tomatoes, cored and cut into eighths
3   tablespoons cornstarch
¼   cup cold water

Season venison strips with pepper. Heat oil in a wok or large skillet over medium-high heat. Add garlic and ginger. Stir-fry 30 seconds. Add venison, and stir-fry for 2 minutes. Add soy sauce, sugar, peppers, cover and cook for 3 minutes. Add tomatoes, cover and cook for 2 minutes. Mix cornstarch with water and stir in a small amount at a time until sauce begins to thicken. Remove from heat and serve with steamed rice.

GRILLED VENISON CHOPS
WITH APRICOT-GINGER SAUCE

*When you are short on time,
try this easy dish.*

6 servings

12   venison chops
¼   cup olive oil
2   teaspoons fresh garlic, minced
1   teaspoon fresh ginger, minced
     or ⅓ teaspoon powdered
     ginger
1   ounce unsalted butter
2   cups beef or game stock
¼   cup orange juice
⅓   cup apricot preserves
2   teaspoons cornstarch mixed
     with 2 teaspoons cold water

SAUCE

In saucepan over medium heat, melt butter and sauté garlic and ginger for 3 to 4 minutes. Add stock, orange juice and apricot preserves and cook over medium-high heat until sauce is reduced to about 1 1/2 cups. Add cornstarch mixture as needed to thicken. Reduce heat to simmer or remove from heat and warm prior to serving.

Brush each venison chop with olive oil and grill on a barbecue or charbroiler until rare to medium rare. Place two chops on each plate and spoon sauce over each.

NEW MEXICO VENISON CHILI

The perfect cure for a winter chill. This version is a bit spicy, so reduce chipotle and/or jalapeño chilies if you prefer a milder version.

6 - 8 servings

1   2 1/2 to 3 pound venison shoulder,
     sirloin or rump roast, cut into
     1 inch cubes
¼   teaspoon salt
½   teaspoon cumin
½   teaspoon chili powder
4   tablespoons olive oil
4   strips smoked bacon, diced
1   large yellow onion, diced
2   Anaheim peppers, seeded and diced
1   medium red bell pepper, seeded
     and chopped
2   jalapeño peppers, seeded and
     diced very fine (see Caution,
     page 46 - Wild Boar Chile Verde)
5   garlic cloves, minced
1   4 ounce can chipotle chiles in
     adobo sauce
¼   teaspoon dried oregano flakes
1   tablespoon ground cumin
¼   teaspoon dried pepper flakes
3   tablespoons chili powder
4   cups canned pinto beans, drained
3   cups canned diced tomatoes,
     drained
¼   cup fresh cilantro, chopped
     salt to taste

In a paper bag or large bowl, toss venison with first 3 ingredients. Heat oil in large skillet over medium heat and brown seasoned meat evenly. Add bacon, cook 3 minutes. Add onion, peppers and garlic. Cook 3 to 4 more minutes or until onions become translucent, but not browned. Transfer contents of skillet to a large stock pot over medium heat and add remaining ingredients except cilantro and salt. Cover and cook until chili begins to bubble, stirring occasionally. Reduce heat to simmer, cover and cook until meat is tender, about 1 ½ hours. Stir in cilantro, season with salt and serve.

SOUPS AND STEWS

Upon returning from a cold, wet day in pursuit of wild game, nothing warms the body better than a heaping bowl of a hearty game stew. If I anticipate spending a long day in the field, I will prepare my soup or stew a day ahead and reheat it upon my return from the hunt. A simmering pot of game stew, a mixed greens salad, and a loaf of warm bread makes a casual and comfortable repast.

Soups and stews are relatively forgiving, and an excellent way for the inexperienced game cook to begin his or her pursuit of wild game cooking superiority. They typically simmer over low temperatures while the meat becomes tender and the flavors blend into an aromatic masterpiece.

While you develop your own signature stock pot creations, there are a few simple rules to follow. Always add the more delicate leafy fresh herbs such as basil, cilantro and parsley about 30 minutes or less before removing the dish from heat. Fresh herbs will lose the majority of their flavors if cooked for extended periods. Hardier herbs such as rosemary, sage and thyme may be added earlier without losing much flavor. With a few exceptions, I prefer to add fresh vegetables about 1 hour or less before the stew or soup is finished. Those who prefer their vegetables less crisp can add fresh vegetables earlier. Stock pots used for cooking stews and soups should be of heavier gauge, rather than thin-walled. Heavy-duty stock pots cook more evenly and are far less likely to burn the ingredients within.

Stews are a good way to make use of odds and ends and tougher cuts of meat; however, make certain that the fat and sinew is carefully trimmed from flesh to avoid the unpleasant taste of gristle and fat. Tip: Many of the following recipes make six or more servings. To prevent waste and spoilage, and have a delicious meal several days (or weeks) later, use your vacuum packaging system and store the pieces in your freezer until needed.

Make use of small quantities of assorted game meats for a unique dish. Keep in mind that large game meats will require more cooking time than upland game and ducks. When cooking with a combination of game animals, it is wise to add delicate game birds after big game cuts have been cooking for awhile. When cooking, do not allow the meat to cook so long that it disintegrates.

Photo at left is fron the recipe on page 58.
Upland Game Bird Chowder

SOUTHWESTERN
SMOKED PHEASANT
SOUP

*A light and flavorful soup, best when
fresh sweet corn is in season.*

6 servings

2 Honey Mustard Smoked Pheasants (see
     page 75), meat pulled from the carcass
     in thin strips
½ cup peanut or corn oil
3 corn tortillas, cut into 1/4 inch strips
½ cup Monterey Jack cheese
1 quart game bird stock or chicken broth
1 tablespoon freshly squeezed lemon juice
¼ teaspoon ground cumin
⅛ teaspoon cayenne pepper
⅓ cup red bell pepper, diced
1 cup raw fresh sweet corn kernels
1 jalapeño pepper, seeded and diced fine
¼ cup fresh cilantro, chopped
    salt and freshly ground black pepper

In a medium sized skillet over medium-high flame, heat oil and fry tortilla strips until crispy. Lay fried tortillas on a sheet pan, sprinkle cheese over and bake in a 350° F oven until cheese is just melted. Remove from oven and cool. In a medium stock pot, heat stock, lemon juice, cumin and cayenne pepper to boil. Add pheasant, bell pepper, corn and jalapeño and cook for 5 minutes. Stir in cilantro, season with salt and pepper. Ladle soup into bowls and garnish with tortilla strips.

HEARTY BOAR SOUP

This soup, inspired by French Master Chef Paul Bocuse, makes good use of boar bones and frequently discarded scraps. If you can hot-smoke the bones and meat rather than roasting them, so much the better!

6 - 8 servings

3-4 pounds wild boar bones and joints with some meat attached
½   pound dried pinto beans, soaked overnight
½   pound dried white or navy beans, soaked overnight
3   quarts water
½   teaspoon salt
¼   teaspoon freshly ground black pepper
1   cup leeks, white part only, washed and diced
1 ½ cups carrot, diced into ¼ inch cubes
1 ½ cups zucchini, diced into ¼ inch cubes
1   cup green beans, strings removed and cut into ½ inch pieces
2   cup potatoes, diced into ½ inch cubes
3 ½ ounces dry small elbow macaroni pasta
6   garlic cloves, minced
1   cup fresh basil leaves
¾   cup olive oil
2   cups ripe tomatoes, peeled, seeded, chopped and drained
    salt and pepper
1   cup Parmesan cheese, freshly grated

Pre-heat oven to 375° F. Place boar pieces in roasting pan and roast in oven until well browned. Place soaked beans, browned boar and water in a large stock pot and bring to a boil. Reduce heat to low, add salt and pepper and simmer for 1 hour while skimming any foam or fat that rises to the surface. Add leeks, carrots, zucchini, green beans and potatoes, and continue simmering for an additional hour. Meanwhile, place 1/2 cup of the liquid from the stock pot, garlic and basil in a food processor or blender. Blend for 10 seconds. While processing at low speed, add the oil in a thin stream until emulsified. Add tomatoes and process for 2 to 3 seconds. Add pasta and cook until tender, about 15 minutes. Remove boar bones. Remove stock pot from heat and stir in mixture from processor. Let stand for 10 minutes. Serve in bowls and top with Parmesan cheese.

RABBIT MULLIGATAWNY SOUP

Always one of my favorite year 'round soups. Try it with light-fleshed game birds as well.

6 to 8 servings

2 cups cottontail rabbit or hare, cut into 1/2 inch cubes
¼ cup flour
1 teaspoon garlic powder
1 teaspoon salt
½ teaspoon freshly ground black pepper
3 tablespoons vegetable oil
¼ cup dry white wine
2 tablespoons butter
½ cup carrots, diced
½ cup celery, diced
⅓ cup red onion, diced
2 teaspoons Madras curry powder
1 quart game bird stock or chicken broth
2 garlic cloves, minced
1 pinch coriander
1 teaspoon freshly grated ginger
⅔ cup Granny Smith apple, diced into 1/4 inch cubes
1 cup cooked rice
½ cup diced tomato
salt and white pepper

Combine flour, garlic powder, salt and ground black pepper. Place in a bag, add rabbit pieces and toss to coat thoroughly. In a medium size stock pot over medium-high flame, heat oil and sauté rabbit until browned. De-glaze pot with wine, scraping any bits from pan. Add butter and sauté carrots, celery and onion for 3 minutes. Sprinkle curry powder over contents of pan and stir to blend. Add stock, garlic, coriander and ginger. Bring to boil, stir and reduce heat to low. Cover and simmer for 20 minutes. Add apple cubes and rice. Cook 6 to 7 minutes more. Add diced tomato and season with salt and white pepper.

RESOLUTION STEW

Guaranteed to bring good luck for the New Year and a great way to utilize a variety of game meats. Stew can be prepared a day or two ahead.

8 - 10 servings

2-3 pounds varietal game meat, waterfowl and/or game birds, boned and cut into bite-sized pieces.
1 cup flour, seasoned with salt and pepper
¼ cup vegetable oil
½ pound bacon slices
2 celery stalks, chopped
1 medium onion, chopped
1 green bell pepper, chopped
2 carrots, diced
1 jalapeño pepper, seeded and finely diced
2 tablespoons garlic cloves, minced
1 16 ounce canned/diced tomatoes, not drained
2 10 ounce packages frozen black-eyed peas
3 cups game stock or beef broth
1 tablespoon Worcestershire sauce
½ teaspoon chili flakes
2 bay leaves
salt and black pepper to taste

Coat game meat with seasoned flour. Heat oil in a large, heavy stock pot and add meat. Cook until evenly browned. Remove meat, add bacon and cook until crispy. Add celery, onions, peppers and carrots until onions become translucent. Add remaining ingredients, cover, and cook over low heat until meat is tender, about 2 to 3 hours.

PORTUGUESE
VENISON STEW

The linguica sausage makes it "Portuguese." If linguica is unavailable, you can substitute one of your favorite spicy pork sausages. Top with garlic croutons.

6 to 8 servings

½	pound linguica sausage, sliced 1/4 inch
1	pound venison stew meat, cubed into 1 inch pieces
½	cup green bell pepper, coarsely chopped
½	cup red bell pepper, coarsely chopped
½	cup red onion, finely chopped
1	cup russet potato, peeled and cubed into 1 inch pieces
3	garlic cloves, minced
4	cups game stock or beef broth
2	cups tomato, diced
1	teaspoon oregano flakes
1	tablespoon fresh rosemary, diced fine
2	bay leaves
½	teaspoon freshly ground black pepper
	salt to taste

In a large stockpot over medium-high heat, cook linguica slices until browned. Add onions and peppers and cook for an additional 3 minutes. Add venison and brown evenly. Stir in potatoes, stock, and garlic. Bring to a boil and reduce heat to simmer. Add oregano, rosemary, bay leaves and pepper. Cover and simmer until venison is tender, about 1 hour, depending on the quality of the meat. Remove bay leaves, add tomato and season with salt as desired.

UPLAND GAME BIRD
CHOWDER

Reminiscent of New England clam chowder, this dish is exceptional with a mixed bag of light-fleshed game birds such as quail, grouse, turkey or pheasant. Serve with warm sourdough bread.

8 servings

3	cups upland game birds, boned and cut into bite-sized pieces
16	slices lean bacon, coarsely chopped
1	cup yellow onion, finely chopped
½	cup green bell pepper, coarsely chopped
1	cup celery, coarsely chopped
1 ½	pounds new red potatoes, skin on and quartered
1	cup game bird stock or chicken broth
1	quart whole milk
1 ½	cups heavy cream
1	tablespoon Worcestershire sauce
1	teaspoon Tabasco sauce or similar hot sauce
	salt and white pepper to taste

In a large saucepan over medium heat, cook the bacon until crisp. Place on paper towels to drain. Discard all but 2 tablespoons of the bacon drippings, and sauté the onion, bell pepper, celery and potatoes for 3 to 4 minutes. Add the game bird pieces and continue to cook until the onions are translucent and the meat is lightly browned. Add the chicken stock, milk, cream and Worcestershire sauce and bring to a boil. Reduce heat to a simmer, add hot sauce. Stir occasionally and cook until the potatoes are tender. Add bacon and season with salt and pepper.

Just Camping

GOURMET CAMP COOKING

As a young boy, I packed provisions for countless hunting and fishing trips in the mountains of Virginia. My experiences taught me to bring along adequate cooking supplies just in case I actually caught a meal. Supplemental food items usually included heavy cans of prepared stews or chili and yes, the often-maligned canned loaf of something made from "pork and pork by-products." Fresh vegetables weren't even considered.

Today, my camp cooking bag contains an assortment of trimmed fresh vegetables, fruit, herbs, pasta, grains and cooking wine that has been decanted into plastic containers. When there is a good likelihood that we will be able to pick up a few birds or catch some fish, I plan menus designed to complement the main ingredient of fish or game. I like to eat trout. Like you, I like it prepared for my tastes. Few meals compare to freshly bagged game or fish, prepared with reasonable care and creativity.

Practically any recipe that can be prepared at home can be tailored to suit the camp cook, including the recipes in this book. If you are camping out of the back of a pickup truck or utility vehicle, there is no excuse for preparing mundane camp fare. A good quality ice cooler will keep it's contents fresh for days and modern camp cooking equipment will handily replace fancy home kitchen appliances. When I am camping by truck or ATV, I carry along my Camp Chef stove. My model has two 30,000 BTU burners and an assortment of accessories that enable me to prepare practically any dish I prepare at home. Once you have used a unit like the Camp Chef, you will wonder how you were able to get along without it. (See the coupon at the back of this book. Mail it

in and the Camp Chef people will send you more information than I can print here about their great stoves). Give me a great propane stove, a cast iron skillet, a few select fresh ingredients and I am in camp-cook heaven.

If you do a great deal of camp cooking, it is a good idea to maintain an inventory of dried herbs, seasonings, bouillon and other assorted non-perishable items. (Check out my Sporting Chef brand. I believe you'll find them indispensable, and extremely flavorable). Professional outfitters know the importance of stocking a constant supply of such items so that only perishable goods need to be purchased prior to departure.

Consider the advantages of thoughtfully planned camp cooked meals. You will save weight, time and frustration by packing smaller units of items that are usually used sparingly. Rather than taking along a large glass bottle of store-bought salad dressing, you could easily prepare a flavorful dressing at home and place it in a plastic container with a tight-fitting lid. To prevent returning home with leftover provisions, I prefer to bring only as much as I can use during a single trip. Planning will also enable the camp cook to spend less time cooking and more time reminiscing about the ones that didn't get away.

A vacuum-packaging machine like the FoodSaver unit is a big plus for the innovative camp chef. Fruits and vegetables can be trimmed, sealed and labeled. Sauces and stocks can be prepared ahead, packaged and frozen. Meats may be trimmed and portioned. Salads and other side dishes can be prepared a day or two ahead and stored for several days. An entire day's meals can be vacuum-packaged providing you with many dishes that can be heated right in the bag while immersed in boiling water. Mixes such as pancake or biscuits can be pre-prepared and vacuum packaged. All you have to do is add the liquid ingredients when ready. Plus vacuum packaging compacts foods, freeing up more space. Vacuum bags are airtight, and don't leak. If you do not have access to such a device, similar results can be achieved by placing items in zipper-lock type bags and gently pressing as much air out as possible before sealing. However, I have found that no matter how carefully I place items in the zipper type bags, they often seem to leak just a bit and can't be used for cooking in water.

When planning menus, try to find multiple uses for most items. Potato flakes can be used to make potato pancakes when paired with flour, eggs, onion and fresh rosemary. Add roasted garlic, powdered milk, and a little butter. Garlic mashed potatoes! Potato flakes are also a good thickening agent for soups, stews and sauces. Cook more pasta than you will need for a side dish at dinner and use the leftovers for a delicious pasta salad the following afternoon. Pack along fresh fruit for breakfast and lunch. Include extra to roll with brown sugar inside prepared pastry dough for a dessert turnover.

If you are not inclined to prepare your own bread and muffin mixes, pick up a box of batter mix to save a few steps. Since a standard oven is usually not available in camp, prepare the batter as directed, add a few fresh herbs, cheese or fruit and cook slowly over a very low flame in a well-oiled skillet covered with a lid or foil. If the heat source is a bit too hot, it may be necessary to flip the bread and brown the top side. The finished product will not be as fluffy as you cook in a conventional oven, but the flavor is just as good assuming that the bread has not been allowed to burn. (You may want to look into getting yourself a Dutch oven. They work great, are easy to clean up and are fun to cook in).

The following menus are designed for ease of production, minimal pack space and of course, high flavor. Shopping and food preparation lists have been included to assist you with your pre-camp planning. Many of the dishes can be prepared at home and transferred to the camp by ice cooler when feasible. If you are the designated camp cook, you can decide how much time you wish to spend preparing meals afield. Chopping vegetables and making sauces is usually easier in a well-equipped kitchen than on the top of a cooler in a twenty mile per hour wind.

Required utensils include a two-burner portable propane camp stove, a grate or screen for cooking over your camp fire, a large skillet, a medium stock pot with lid and assorted tongs, eating and mixing spoons and spatulas. I personally prefer well-seasoned cast iron skillets and Dutch ovens to lighter-gauge pots and pans, but often they are too heavy for pack trips. Pack non-perishable items within large pots to take advantage of all available space.

All menus are designed to feed six hungry adults. Recipes specifying freshly bagged fish or game may require substitutions on less successful outings.

BLUE RIDGE DEER CAMP

Camping by truck or jeep in the fall means crisp nights and gorgeous fall colors. The Blue Ridge Mountains of Virginia are plentiful with white-tailed deer, wild turkeys, ruffed grouse and trout, all of which make for excellent camping fare. The following menus and recipes do not include game meats, but any freshly bagged game would make a welcome substitution. Fall produce includes crisp apples, late sweet corn and an assortment of squash. Stop by a fruit and vegetable stand on the way to your destination and pick out just-picked firm, ripe produce. Smithfield ham, one source of Virginia's culinary pride, is used for preparing breakfast, lunch and dinner. If Smithfield ham is unavailable in your area, substitute with another well-cured salty smoked ham.

Breakfast
Ham and Tomato Scramble
Apple Tart

Lunch
Corn Chowder

Dinner
Smithfield Ham with Redeye Gravy
Black-Eyed Peas
Country Coleslaw
Cheddar Corn Bread
Chocolate-Pecan Cluster

SHOPPING/PREP LIST

- 1 5 pound Smithfield ham
- 3 medium red onions
- 2 celery stalks
- 3 medium carrots
- 1 green bell pepper
- 1 large baking potato
- 3 ears corn, (or 2 cups canned corn)
- 3 apples
- 1 large head green cabbage, shredded and sealed in a zipper lock type bag or vacuum-sealed bag
- ½ pound butter
- 12 large eggs, shells removed, beaten and placed in a secure container
- 1 14 ounce can diced tomatoes
- 2 pound can black-eyed peas

- 1 cup cheddar cheese, grated
- 2 cups cornmeal
- 8 ounces semi-sweet chocolate
- ½ pound pecan pieces
- 1 prepared pastry dough
- ½ cup shortening
- 2 cups self-rising flour
- 5 tablespoons water

Cut shortening into flour, add water and mix to form dough. Knead until smooth and wrap with plastic wrap.

- 1 prepared coleslaw dressing
- ½ cup white wine vinegar
- 1 tablespoon sugar
- 1 teaspoon salt
- ⅓ cup salad oil

Combine all ingredients in a tight-fitting jar and shake vigorously to blend.

- 1 quart vegetable oil
- ½ cup flour
- 4 cans condensed milk
- 4 chicken bouillon cubes
- 1 teaspoon coffee for brewing salt, pepper, chili flakes and white sugar

EQUIPMENT

2	large skillets
1	Dutch oven or large heavy stockpot
1	medium sauce pan
1	large bowl
1	tongs
1	spatula
1	soup ladle
	Waxed paper, aluminum foil

RECIPES:

HAM AND TOMATO SCRAMBLE

Remove outside crust of ham and prepare 2 cups of diced center-cut ham. Cut one onion in half and dice. Melt 2 tablespoons butter in a large skillet and sauté ham and onions for 3 minutes over medium-high heat. Add 3 cups beaten eggs and stir until set. Mix in drained diced tomatoes, season with salt and pepper and serve.

SMITHFIELD HAM WITH REDEYE GRAVY

Scrub ham and slice into 18 thin slices (allowing 3 slices per camper). Coat a large skillet with vegetable oil and fry ham slices on both sides until lightly browned. Wrap ham in foil and keep in a warm location. Add ¾ cup water, ¾ cup brewed coffee and ¼ cup condensed milk to skillet. Heat to boil over high heat, scraping the bottom of the pan to loosen bits of ham, until liquid is slightly thickened. Pour gravy over ham.

CHOCOLATE PECAN CLUSTER

Melt chocolate in sauce pan over low heat, stirring constantly. Remove from heat and add pecans, stir to blend. Drop from a teaspoon onto waxed paper. Allow to cool until set.

CORN CHOWDER

Prepare the chowder before leaving camp in the morning or the night before.

Dice 1 onion, 2 celery stalks, 2 carrots and 1 baking potato. Remove the kernels from 3 ears of fresh corn (or use 2 cups of canned corn). Add 2 cups of diced ham and ¼ cup vegetable oil to a large pot or Dutch oven and cook over medium heat for 3 to 5 minutes until ham is lightly browned. Add diced onion, celery and carrots. Stir into pot and cook for 4 to 5 minutes or until onion is translucent. Stir in 2 tablespoons flour and cook until flour is blended into ham and vegetables and no lumps are visible. Add potatoes, 3 cups water, 2 cups condensed milk and 4 bouillon cubes. Simmer over low heat until potatoes are tender. Stir in corn, season with salt and pepper and cook for 3 minutes more.

BLACK-EYED PEAS

In a medium pot, add 2 tablespoons vegetable oil and heat over medium heat. Add 1 diced carrot, ½ diced red onion, ½ cup diced ham and ½ teaspoon chili flakes. Cook, stirring occasionally, for 3 to 5 minutes. Add black-eyed peas and heat to serving temperature.

COUNTRY COLESLAW

Combine shredded coleslaw with ½ cup diced bell pepper, ½ thin-sliced red onion and 1 apple, finely diced. Toss in a large bowl with prepared coleslaw dressing.

APPLE TART

Pull a piece from the prepared pastry dough and flatten it into a circle about ¼ inch thick and 5 inches in diameter. Dice 2 apples into ¼ inch cubes. Place a small amount of apples on the center of the pastry circle, sprinkle sugar over apples and fold pastry over, pressing down firmly to seal edges. In a large skillet, add enough oil to coat the bottom about ¼ inch. Heat oil over medium-high heat until very hot. Fry both sides of each tart until golden brown, turning with metal tongs or spatula. Serve with butter. Reserve cooled oil for lunch and dinner preparation.

CHEDDAR CORN BREAD

Combine cornmeal, 2 tablespoons sugar, ½ cup beaten eggs, 1 cup condensed milk and ¼ cup vegetable oil in a bowl. Mix well. Add 1 cup grated cheddar cheese. Pour mixture into a well-greased large skillet, cover and cook over very low heat for 8 to 10 minutes. Check bottom of cornbread. If browned, flip bread over and brown other side, covered, for an additional 6 to 8 minutes.

EASY SUMMERTIME CAMP

For me, the best time of year is when the main objective is to get some fresh air, take a day or two off from the daily grind and get in some bonus fishing. Take advantage of summer fresh fruits and vegetables, and prepare a healthy menu for you and your guests. Most of the preparation is done at home to save time so you may enjoy the beautiful weather. You can save even more time by preparing the Sweet and Sour Chicken Brochette at home, cooking within 24 hours of preparation.

Breakfast
Orange Flavored French Toast with Maple Syrup

Lunch
Assorted Cold Cuts and Cheeses
Fresh Fruit Salad

Dinner
Sweet and Sour Chicken Brochette
Caesar Salad
Baked Potato
Chocolate-Nut Banana

½   pound sliced ham
½   pound sliced turkey
½   pound sliced roast beef
¼   pound sliced sharp cheddar cheese
¼   pound sliced Swiss cheese
¼   pound grated Parmesan cheese
4   oranges
8   bananas, slightly green
1   pineapple, peeled and cored
1   cantaloupe, peeled, seeds removed and cut into 4 wedges
1   honeydew melon, peeled, seeds removed and cut into 4 wedges
1   loaf thick-sliced buttermilk bread
2   French bread loaves
½   cup mayonnaise
½   cup whole grain mustard
1   medium can whole pitted black olives
2   large whole dill pickles
2   pounds boneless chicken breasts, skin removed
1   red bell pepper, seeded and cut into 12 pieces

SHOPPING/PREP LIST

1   red onion, skin removed and cut into quarters
6   medium baking potatoes
2   heads romaine lettuce
½   pound butter
3   eggs, shells removed, beaten and placed in a container with a secure lid
6   Hershey's chocolate bars
1   cup roasted peanuts
1   can condensed milk
2   cups maple syrup
    salt, pepper and white sugar

Prepared Caesar Dressing
1   garlic clove
2   anchovies
1   egg
1   tablespoon red wine vinegar
1   tablespoon Worcestershire sauce
2   teaspoons lemon juice
½   cup olive oil

In a blender or food processor, add first 6 ingredients and process until blended. While motor is running, add oil in a thin stream until dressing thickens.

Place in a secure container and keep refrigerated.

Prepared Sweet & Sour Basting Sauce
⅔   cup pineapple juice
⅔   cup white wine vinegar
3   tablespoons vegetable oil
3   tablespoons brown sugar
2   tablespoons soy sauce
½   teaspoon black pepper
1   tablespoon cornstarch mixed with 2 T cold water

Combine first 6 ingredients in a sauce pan and bring to boil. Add cornstarch mixture, a little at a time, stirring until thickened. Cool and place in a secure container and keep refrigerated.

EQUIPMENT

- 1 large skillet
- 1 cheese grater
- 12 bamboo skewers
- 1 grill or screen for campfire cooking
- 1 long metal tongs
- 1 serving spoon
- 1 roll heavy-duty aluminum foil
- 2 large bowls
- 1 large platter

RECIPES:

ORANGE FLAVORED FRENCH TOAST WITH MAPLE SYRUP

Combine beaten eggs, 3/4 teaspoon salt, 2 tablespoons sugar, condensed milk and the juice of 2 oranges. Dip 2 to 3 bread slices per person in mixture and fry in a little butter in a medium-hot skillet. Serve with maple syrup.

ASSORTED COLD CUTS AND CHEESES

Remove outside leaves from romaine lettuce heads and arrange on a large platter. Slice cheddar and Swiss cheeses. Slice pickles into 4 spears each. Slice 1 1/2 of French bread loaves diagonally. Save remaining 1/2 loaf. Arrange on platter with sliced meat. Garnish with 1/2 of black olives. Serve with mustard and mayonnaise.

FRESH FRUIT SALAD

Cut pineapple in half. Reserve one half and cut the other half into 1 inch cubes. Peel remaining 2 oranges and slice into 6 slices each.

Cut cantaloupe and honeydew melons into bite-sized pieces. Peel and cut 2 bananas into bite-sized pieces. Toss cut fruit gently in a large bowl and serve.

SWEET AND SOUR CHICKEN BROCHETTE

Soak bamboo skewers in water for 30 minutes or more. Cut chicken into 18 pieces, approximately 2 ounces each. Cut remaining pineapple into 1 inch cubes. Break up onion quarters into smaller pieces. Alternately load bamboo skewers with an onion, red bell pepper, chicken and pineapple. Place on a grill or screen over a medium-hot campfire and baste with sweet and sour basting sauce while cooking. Serve when chicken is thoroughly cooked.

CAESAR SALAD

Slice remaining French loaf into thin slices, brush with butter and toast on both sides over campfire. Chop or tear romaine lettuce into large pieces and place in a large bowl with grated Parmesan cheese, remaining black olives, toasted bread slices and prepared Caesar dressing. Toss to coat with dressing and serve immediately.

BAKED POTATO

Wrap potatoes with 3 layers of "crinkled" foil and place in a bed of campfire coals, turning frequently with long tongs. Cooking time is approximately 1 hour. Remove foil and serve with butter.

CHOCOLATE-NUT BANANA

Peel 6 bananas and slice each lengthwise without cutting all of the way through the bananas. Open each banana at the hinge and place on a piece of aluminum foil. Break apart chocolate bars and place in banana opening along with nuts. Carefully fold banana and wrap with foil. Place on grill or screen until chocolate is melted. Serve immediately.

HIGH COUNTRY ELK CAMP

Getting there on horseback can be quite a journey. Most established high camps come equipped with cast iron cooking vessels and a large Dutch oven. A collapsible two-burner propane unit is also fairly common. Lunch can be made at breakfast and carried in a day pack while stalking a trophy bull elk. It's a good idea to pre-cook items such as potatoes, carrots, pasta and any other item that requires boiling water, and vacuum-package them before heading up the mountain. Anyone who has waited for water to boil at high altitudes appreciates any reduction of cooking time.

Breakfast
Canadian Bacon, Cheese and Fresh Sage Omelette
Homestyle Potatoes
Orange Segments

Lunch
Bacon, Lettuce and Tomato Burrito
Apple
Candy Bar

Dinner
Cheese Quesadilla Appetizer
Elk (or beef) Burgundy
Orange and Onion Salad
High Country Biscuits and Herb Butter
Apple Turnover

SHOPPING/PREP LIST

2 pounds Canadian Bacon, sliced into 1 ounce slices
3 pounds elk or beef stew meat, cut into 1 inch cubes
1 dozen eggs, shells removed and placed in a container with a secure lid
1 pound sharp cheddar cheese, grated
1 pound peppered Monterey Jack cheese, grated
4 baking potatoes
4 medium red onions, diced
1 green bell pepper, chopped
3 navel oranges
8 apples
1 head iceberg lettuce
1 pound fresh mushrooms
10 10 inch flour tortillas
6 garlic cloves

2 cups burgundy wine
2 beef bouillon cubes
1 package egg noodles
1 bunch fresh sage, stems removed (or substitute 2 tablespoons dried sage)
2 14 ½ ounce cans diced tomato, drained and repacked in a secure plastic container
1 6 ounce can tomato paste
¾ pound butter
¼ cup cornstarch
1 tube prepared turnover dough

2 cups flour, mixed with 4 teaspoons baking powder, 1/2 teaspoon salt and 5 tablespoons solid shortening
1 can condensed milk
1 can Mandarin orange segments
½ cup brown sugar
6 candy bars
2 bay leaves
1 small can sliced black olives
1 small can cooking spray
salt, pepper and dried thyme

Prepared Salad Dressing
3 tablespoons red wine vinegar
⅓ cup olive oil,
1 teaspoon dijon mustard
dash salt and pepper

Mix and place in a secure container.

EQUIPMENT

2	large skillets
1	large stock pot or Dutch oven
1	large bowl
1	medium rubber spatula
1	serving spoon
1	serving tongs

RECIPES:

CANADIAN BACON, CHEESE AND FRESH SAGE OMELETTE

Dice 8 slices of Canadian bacon. In a large bowl, combine bacon, eggs, ½ pound cheddar cheese, ½ pound peppered Jack cheese, ¼ cup sage and pinch of salt and pepper. Stir to mix and break up eggs. Melt butter in a large skillet over medium-low heat. Add egg mixture and heat, stirring often until eggs set. Remove from heat, place plate over skillet and turn skillet over to put omelette on plate. Cut omelette into 6 equal wedges.

BACON, LETTUCE AND TOMATO BURRITO

Brown both sides of 18 slices of Canadian bacon. Lay 3 slices out on each of 6 flour tortillas. Top with lettuce, black olives and well-drained diced tomatoes. Fold bottom and top edges over mixture and roll up burrito tightly. Place in zipper-lock bag or wrap with plastic wrap.

ORANGE AND ONION SALAD

In a large bowl, combine remaining lettuce (chopped), onions and mandarin oranges, drained. Toss with prepared dressing.

HIGH COUNTRY BISCUITS

Soften ¼ pound butter and blend in a pinch of dried thyme and ¼ cup fresh sage, minced. Roll mixture in plastic or foil and cool to set. Add flour mixture to a large bowl. Using two knives, cut solid shortening into flour mixture until mixture resembles coarse cornmeal. Mix in 1 cup of canned milk until just mixed. Heat a large skillet over very low heat, coat with cooking spray and drop equal portions of mixture onto skillet. Cover with lid or foil and cook for 10 minutes or until lightly browned. Serve with herb butter.

HOMESTYLE POTATOES

Dice potatoes into ½ inch cubes. Mince 2 garlic cloves. Spray a large skillet with cooking spray and melt a small amount of butter over medium-high heat to coat pan. Add potatoes, onions and bell pepper. Spray contents of skillet with cooking spray to coat evenly. Cook until medium, brown, stirring often. Stir in ½ can of tomato paste. Season with salt and pepper.

APPLE TURNOVERS

Dice 2 apples into ¼ inch cubes. Add to skillet over medium heat. Add remaining butter and sauté for 3 minutes. Add brown sugar and stir in until sugar begins to dissolve. Transfer contents to bowl and allow to cool. Clean skillet and spray with cooking spray. Cut a slit in each of 6 prepared turnover dough pieces and stuff with equal portions of apple mixture. Cook over very low heat, covered, until lightly browned.

ELK BURGUNDY

Cooking this main dish works well on a bed of hot coals in a Dutch oven.

Fill stock pot ¾ with water, add a pinch or two of salt and bring to boil. Cook pasta until cooked, but firm (al dente). Remove pasta, toss with a little butter and set aside. Cut remaining Canadian bacon into thin strips. Spray stock pot with cooking spray and add enough butter to just coat pot. Heat stock pot over medium heat, add bacon and cook until lightly browned. Add elk meat, season with a little salt and a lot of pepper. Cook, stirring occasionally until elk meat is evenly browned. Add wine, two cups water and bouillon cubes. Bring to boil. Add remaining tomato paste, minced garlic cloves, 1 cup of red onion, a pinch or two of dried thyme and bay leaves. Cook until meat begins to soften and break apart, about 2 hours. Add mushrooms. Cook 5 minutes more. Mix cornstarch with equal part cold water. Add to stock pot, stirring in a little at a time, until thickened. Add cooked pasta to pot to warm. Season with salt and pepper and serve.

CHEESE QUESADILLA

In a large ungreased skillet over medium heat, lay 1 flour tortilla in skillet, top with ½ of remaining cheeses and any remaining diced tomatoes. Lay another tortilla over cheese. When cheese begins to melt, carefully flip tortillas over and continue to cook until cheese has melted. Remove from pan, slice into wedges and repeat process with remaining tortillas and cheese.

HELL'S CANYON BOAT CAMP

The following menus are from a combination of fishing and bird hunting trips on the Snake River in Hell's Canyon, on the Idaho-Oregon border. The game of choice is Chukar and Hungarian partridge. These bird recipes work equally well with quail, grouse, pheasant and any other upland game birds. A cottontail rabbit or two will also suffice as a substitution for game birds, but make certain that they are thoroughly cooked and that you wash your hands carefully after cleaning. Cooking may be done on either a propane stove or an open campfire.

Breakfast
Apple-Raisin Pancakes
Grilled Ham with Pineapple Glaze

Lunch
Chukar Salad Sandwich
Corn Tortilla Chips and Tomato Salsa

Dinner
Camp-Smoked Trout Hors d'oeuvre with Guacamole Grilled Chukar and Hungarian Partridge with Apple-Rosemary Sauce
Grilled Vegetables – Stir-Fried Rice
Sourdough Parmesan Garlic Bread
Raisin-Nut Cookie

SHOPPING/PREP LIST

1 ½ pounds lean smoked ham,
        cut into eight 3 ounce slices
3 Granny Smith apples
4 sprigs fresh rosemary (or
        3 tablespoons dried
        rosemary leaves)
½ bunch fresh parsley
1 firm avocado
2 medium zucchini
4 carrots
1 medium yellow onion
2 green onions
4 celery stalks
2 lemons
4 garlic cloves
½ cup sour cream
½ pound butter
1 cup crushed pineapple
2 14 ounce cans tomato salsa, or
        4 cups fresh tomato salsa
1 small can apple juice

1 cup dry white wine
3 eggs, beaten, shells removed
        and placed in a container
        with a secure lid
2 cups evaporated milk
1 cup vegetable oil
1 cup honey
3 sourdough baguettes
        (or other French-style loaf)
1 cup low-fat mayonnaise
⅔ cup dijon mustard
1 large bag tortilla chips
3 cups cooked white rice
¼ cup brown sugar
¼ cup soy sauce
    salt and pepper

Prepared Pancake Mix
2 cup flour
3 teaspoons baking powder
1 cup raisins
¼ cup sugar
1 teaspoon salt

Prepared Cookie Mix
1 cup each walnut pieces & raisins
2 cups flour
1 teaspoon each salt & cinnamon
½ teaspoon baking soda
2 cups oats
¾ cup sugar

Prepared Trout "Brine"
⅔ cup brown sugar
¾ cup salt
1 teaspoon each ground cloves,
        onion powder, garlic powder,
        ground allspice

EQUIPMENT

- 2 large skillets
- 1 medium sauce pan
- 1 grill or screen for campfire cooking
- 1 large bowl
- 1 set tongs
- 1 spatula
- 1 roll heavy-duty aluminum foil

RECIPES:

APPLE-RAISIN PANCAKES

In a large bowl, combine 2/3 of beaten eggs, pancake mix, 1 apple (diced), 2 cups evaporated milk and 1/3 cup vegetable oil. Lightly coat a large skillet with vegetable oil and heat over medium heat. Drop 2 - 3 tablespoons of batter onto skillet and brown on both sides. Serve immediately.

GRILLED HAM WITH PINEAPPLE GLAZE

Combine 1/4 cup honey with crushed pineapple. Place 6 ham slices in a large skillet over medium heat, brown one side, flip each slice and top with pineapple-honey mixture. Brown bottom side and serve.

CHUKAR SALAD SANDWICH

Remove the breasts from 6 to 8 chukar, season with salt and pepper and cook in a lightly oiled skillet until just cooked. Remove the leaves from 1 sprig of rosemary and dice fine with 1/4 cup fresh parsley leaves. Dice 2 celery stalks. Add chukar, herbs and celery to 1/2 cup mayonnaise and 1/4 cup dijon mustard and blend well. Season with salt and pepper. Cut 2 of the baguettes into 6 pieces, slice in half and fill with salad mixture.

CORN TORTILLA CHIPS WITH TOMATO SALSA

Allot 1/2 of the bag of tortilla chips and 2/3 of the salsa for lunch.

GRILLED VEGETABLES

Slice zucchini and 2 of the carrots lengthwise into 3 slices. Slice 1/2 of an onion into 3 slices. Brush vegetables with vegetable oil and season with salt and pepper. Place on grate and grill over hot coals until just browned on both sides.

STIR-FRIED RICE

Finely dice 2 carrots, 2 celery stalks and 1/2 onion. Add oil to a large skillet over medium-high heat. Sauté vegetables for 2 to 3 minutes, add 2 cups cooked rice and 1/4 cup soy sauce. Stir-fry until hot. Season with pepper.

SOURDOUGH GARLIC BREAD

Combine 3/4 cup butter with 1/4 cup mayonnaise, 4 minced garlic cloves and chopped parsley. Slice 1 sourdough baguette lengthwise and spread mixture evenly over both sides of bread. Wrap with foil and place over campfire on grill, turning frequently to prevent burning. Remove from foil, slice and serve.

RAISIN-NUT COOKIE

Combine remaining 3/4 cup honey, 3/4 cup butter, remaining 1/3 of beaten eggs and mix to blend. Add cookie mix and drop by rounded tablespoons onto a lightly buttered skillet over very low heat. Cover with lid or foil and cook for 5 minutes or until lightly browned on bottom. Flip and cook, covered, for an additional 4 to 6 minutes until other side is lightly browned.

CAMP-SMOKED TROUT

Clean and pat-dry 2 to 3 small to medium trout. Rub inside and out with brine mixture. Place in a plastic bag and keep cool for 3 to 6 hours. Remove from bag, shake off excess brine. Place grill or screen 1 foot above hot coals. Add oak, mesquite, fruitwood or other hardwood pieces over coals. Note: Look for hardwood as you cruise around by boat. Make "tent" out of aluminum foil large enough to cover fish, forming a peak in the center. Cut a hole in the peak of the tent. Place trout on screen, cover with tent and add wood pieces as necessary to keep smoke coming from coals. Depending on the amount of heat from the fire, smoking should take about 1 hour or less. The less the heat, the greater the smoke flavor. When smoked fish is cooked, peel back skin, remove bones and reserve meat. Combine avocado, 1/4 cup mayonnaise, juice of 1 lemon and remaining salsa and mash to make a paste. Spoon a teaspoon or so of guacamole paste onto tortilla chip and top with a small piece of smoked trout.

GRILLED CHUKAR AND HUNGARIAN PARTRIDGE

Baste birds with remaining dijon mustard and season with salt and pepper. Grill over hot coals until just cooked. To test for doneness, prick the meaty part of the thigh. Thigh juices will run clear when cooked. Dice green onions and add to sauce pan with apple juice, white wine and juice of 1 lemon. Cook over high heat, uncovered until reduced by one-half. Peel and dice remaining 2 apples and add to liquid with 3 sprigs rosemary. Cook for 5 to 7 minutes over medium heat. Remove rosemary, add 1/4 cup brown sugar and stir in 1/2 cup sour cream. Heat, stirring constantly, but do not boil. Pour sauce over cooked birds.

COOKING WITH SMOKE

Imparting a smoke flavor to game meats can be accomplished by either completely cooking the meat within the smoker, or by flavoring with smoke for a brief period of time, usually about 30 minutes or so, and then finishing the dish in a conventional oven. I prefer the latter method as game has a tendency to dry out with prolonged cooking. Electric and briquet water smokers which have become popular in recent years will help to protect lean game meats by adding additional moisture to the smoking process, but I still like the controlled temperature of an oven.

Choice of wood for smoking is a matter of personal preference. I like fruit wood, which is found in abundance in many areas of the United States. I've had good luck with pear wood. You can purchase chips or chunks of wood, or gather green wood and chop them into small pieces yourself.

If you do not have a conventional smoker, you can utilize your gas grill or barbecue kettle with surprisingly good results. Put a handful or two of wood chips which have been soaked in water for 30 minutes in a disposable foil pan and place the pan directly on the lava rock on one side of the gas grill. Set the meat to be smoked over the pan as the wood chips begin to smoke. Since removing a hot barbecue grate can be an unnerving experience, you may not be able to finish the meat with smoke, but the flavor of smoke will permeate the flesh. In a barbecue kettle, spread ash-white hot coals around the sides of the bottom grate and sprinkle soaked wood chips over the coals. Place the meat in the center of the grill, away from direct heat and place the lid over the kettle.

I have enjoyed some outstanding meats cooked in makeshift smokers made from 50 gallon metal drums. A fire box is constructed out of metal around the outside of the opening. The heat is controlled by partially opening or closing the lid. The fire box is stoked with a mixture of green and seasoned pear wood. The smoke and fire is drawn into the drum by the draft created by the top opening. A group of close friends host an annual free duck feed where 200 ducks are slow-cooked in such contraptions with excellent results. Everyone contributes a duck or two and a raffle is held to raise money for the next year's side dishes and beverages. The birds are seasoned only with salt and pepper, yet the flavor and tenderness is sensational.

Experience and personal preference will tell you when to remove meat from smoke. Keep in mind that you can always finish an underdone game dish in an oven or by placing it back in the smoker. Over-smoked game will dry out much as it does with other cooking methods. The resulting meat will be tough and chewy and may taste more like charcoal than wild game.

Experiment with smoking any game for 15 minutes with a heavy smoke prior to preparing as specified in other recipes. Game stews and roasts will greatly benefit from the smoky flavor, recalling the aroma of camp cooking after a long day afield. Smoke seasoned game birds make an excellent salad tossed with crisp mixed greens, sunflower seeds and a fresh raspberry vinaigrette. The many uses of smoked game is limited only by your imagination.

GARLIC SMOKED
WILD TURKEY

I have a weakness for garlic. Lots of garlic. If you are not quite so inclined, reduce the portion of garlic in this recipe accordingly. The vegetables will add a little moisture during prolonged smoking and can be served as a side dish. Carve the meat from the smoked bird and serve with Grilled Red Bell Pepper Sauce (see page 87).

4 servings

10	garlic cloves
1	yellow onion, quartered
2	celery stalks, cut into 2 inch pieces
1	carrot, cut into 1 inch pieces
2	tablespoons fresh parsley, minced
2	bay leaves
½	teaspoon salt
¼	teaspoon freshly ground black pepper
¼	cup olive oil
1	large tom turkey, skin intact
4	strips smoked bacon

Stuff turkey with onion, celery, carrot, parsley, bay leaves and 2 cloves of garlic. Cut in half. Truss legs. Mince 6 garlic cloves and combine with salt, pepper and olive oil. Rub mixture over turkey and refrigerate for 2 to 3 hours. Mince remaining 2 garlic cloves and add to water pan in water smoker or to a water pan added to a dry smoker, close to the heat source. Place bacon over turkey breast and smoke at approximately 150°F for 4 to 5 hours or until breast meat close to the rib cage reaches 145°F. Remove bacon and let stand for 15 minutes before carving.

SMOKED BOAR TENDERLOIN
WITH BALSAMIC CHERRY SAUCE

This preparation works best with a barbecue kettle with hot coals seasoned with soaked fruit wood chips. Skewer large earthy mushrooms and add to the barbecue about half way through the cooking process for a great side dish.

4 servings

3	garlic cloves
1	teaspoon freshly ground black pepper
½	teaspoon ground allspice
¼	cup brown sugar
2	pounds, boar tenderloins, trimmed of fat and sinew
1	cup Balsamic Cherry Sauce (see page 86)

Combine first 4 ingredients and rub over tenderloins. Cover and refrigerate for 3 to 4 hours. Soak 3 cups fruit wood chips in water for 30 minutes. Prepare sauce and keep warm. Place briquettes or wood chunks to one side of barbecue and burn until coals are ash-white. Drain wood chips and sprinkle over coals. Wait until wood chips begin to smoke. Place lightly greased grill over coals, leave vents open just a bit and place tenderloins on grill, away from coals. Smoke for 10 minutes and then move tenderloins over coals. Cook until medium or until internal temperature reaches 140°F. For each serving, slice tenderloin into 1/4 inch slices, arrange on plate and spoon sauce over half of slices.

SMOKED DUCK
WITH A CITRUS GLAZE

Try this preparation with a trio of plump drake mallard, canvasback or black ducks. There is actually enough marinade for a few more ducks if you have a surplus or a big appetite. Perhaps you could smoke a couple of extra birds for a sandwich or salad during the week.

6 servings

4-6	large ducks, skin intact
1	cup orange juice
1	cup grapefruit juice
¼	cup freshly squeezed lemon juice
¼	cup freshly squeezed lime juice
1	cup dry white wine
½	cup soy sauce
2	dashes Tabasco
½	cup brown sugar
2	teaspoons fresh ginger, minced
½	teaspoon ground coriander
¼	teaspoon white pepper
½	teaspoon freshly ground black pepper
¼	cup maple syrup
½	cup orange marmalade
2	large navel oranges, peeled and cut into wedges
3-4	sprigs fresh cilantro

Rinse ducks inside and out with cold water and pat dry with paper towels. Combine next 11 ingredients, stir to mix well and pour over ducks. Cover and refrigerate 12 to 24 hours. Remove ducks from marinade and air dry for 1 hour. Transfer marinade to a large sauce pan over medium-high heat and reduce liquid to 1 cup. Add black pepper, maple syrup and marmalade and heat to blend ingredients. Smoke ducks with low heat (125° F or less) for 2 hours. Transfer to a baking dish.

Baste with a little sauce, reserving about 1 cup, and bake in a 425° F oven for 6 to 8 minutes until skin is crisp and internal temperature is 135° F to 140°F. Remove ducks from oven and let stand for 5 minutes. Carve breasts from breastbone and remove legs and thighs. Slice breasts diagonally into 1/2 inch slices. Arrange sliced breasts around the outside edges of a large serving platter. Place legs in the center of the platter, garnish platter with oranges and cilantro and serve with warmed reserved sauce.

ANGEL HAIR PASTA
WITH SMOKED DUCK AND MUSHROOMS

Thin-sliced smoked duck team up with delicate angel hair pasta and fresh mushrooms. Although the recipe does not specify a particular type of mushroom, use the more earthy and flavorful varieties such as portabella, porcini, chanterelle or morel.

4 servings

4 - 6	large smoked boneless duck breasts, skin intact and sliced diagonally into ¼ inch thick strips
1	tablespoon olive oil
4	tablespoons butter
1	shallot, finely diced
2	garlic cloves, minced
2	cups fresh mushrooms, hard part of stems removed and stems and caps sliced thick
1	cup game bird stock or chicken broth
¼	cup fresh parsley, minced
½	cup tomatoes, seeded and diced
	salt and freshly ground black pepper to taste
5	cups hot, cooked angel hair pasta freshly grated Parmesan cheese

Heat olive oil and 2 tablespoons of butter in a large skillet over medium heat. Add shallot and garlic, sauté 2 to 3 minutes. Add mushrooms and sauté until they release juices. Add game bird stock, increase heat to medium-high and cook, uncovered for 5 minutes. Add duck, parsley and tomatoes. Stir to warm. Remove from heat and stir in remaining 2 tablespoons butter. Serve over pasta and garnish with cheese.

HERB AND SPICE
SMOKED DOVES

I like to hot-smoke small birds such as doves, quail, huns and chukar. If your smoker only smokes at lower temperatures, smoke the birds for 1 hour and finish in a very hot oven or barbecue for 3 to 4 minutes.

4 servings

12 doves, skin intact
⅓ cup kosher salt
⅔ cup firmly packed brown sugar
1 teaspoon ground cloves
1 teaspoon ground allspice
1 teaspoon onion powder
1 teaspoon garlic powder
½ teaspoon ground cinnamon
¼ cup fresh rosemary, minced
2 tablespoons fresh sage, minced
2 tablespoons fresh thyme, minced

Rinse doves with cold water and pat dry with paper towels. Combine remaining ingredients and rub birds, inside and out with mixture. Cover and refrigerate for 24 hours. Remove birds from refrigerator, place on a rack and air dry for 2 to 3 hours. Place in a hot smoker (325° F to 350° F) or barbecue kettle with soaked wood chips and cook for 3 to 4 minutes per side or until juices run clear when thigh meat is pricked. Internal temperature should not exceed 145° F.

GOOSE JERKY

Comparing the taste of a delicious plump Canada Honker to a lean Snow Goose is like comparing filet mignon to hamburger. I would usually choose hamburger over the Snow Goose. To make them edible however, I turn Snow Geese into jerky. This recipe works very well with other species, too.

4 goose breast halves, skin, silver skin and all gristle removed and sliced across the "grain" into 1/4 inch thick strips
1 cup Worcestershire sauce
½ cup low-salt soy sauce
6 garlic cloves, minced
2 teaspoons fresh ginger, grated (optional)
¼ cup Balsamic vinegar
½ cup honey or 2/3 cup brown sugar
¼ cup cracked black pepper
2 tablespoons chili flakes

Thoroughly rinse sliced goose strips with cold water and drain well. Combine remaining ingredients in a sauce pan and heat to blend flavors and dissolve honey or sugar. Cool marinade and toss in a large bowl with goose strips. Cover and refrigerate for 12 hours, tossing occasionally to marinate evenly. Remove meat from marinade. Lay on a rack or screen in a smoker with low heat (below 125° F) and smoke for 8 to 10 hours or until jerky is thoroughly dried. Cool and store in a jar with a tight-fitting lid or a FoodSaver vacuum sealed bag. Jerky may also be frozen indefinitely and thawed as needed.

Note: Jerky can be prepared without a smoker by laying the marinated strips on a sheet pan and baking at very low temperature in a conventional oven for about 4 to 5 hours..

SMOKED PHEASANT
WITH PISTACHIO PESTO CREAM SAUCE

The birds are flavored, not fully cooked in the smoker and then sautéed to retain moisture. Great with angel hair pasta.

6 - 8 servings

Pistachio Pesto Cream Sauce (see page 87)

    4   pheasants, halved with skin intact

Prior to smoking, marinate the pheasants in the following:
- 2 cups water
- 2 cups dry white wine
- 1 cup soy sauce
- 6 garlic cloves, minced
- ½ teaspoon sesame oil
- ½ cup green onions, diced fine
- 1 cup brown sugar
- 2 lemons, juiced

Mix in a very large bowl or tub and add pheasant halves, coating all surfaces with marinade. Cover and refrigerate for 10 to 12 hours, turning pheasants every 3 hours. Remove from marinade and air dry in a cool place for 2 to 3 hours prior to smoking. Smoke for 2 hours with low heat and your favorite fruit wood. Remove from smoker and carefully remove meat from bones, keeping meat pieces and skin intact.

Prepare Pistachio Pesto Cream Sauce found in the Game Sauces section of this book.

Sauté smoked meat in a large skillet with 2 tablespoons olive oil, 1/4 cup white wine and 1 teaspoon minced fresh garlic until just cooked. Meat should be a little pink. Slice breasts and thighs and arrange around pasta. Spoon sauce over pheasant slices.

HONEY MUSTARD
SMOKED PHEASANT

This sweet smoked pheasant is great as an appetizer, cubed in a salad or sliced and sauced as an entrée. Smoked pheasants can be wrapped tightly or vacuum-sealed and frozen for up to 6 months.

Requires 4 pheasants

- 2 cups dry white wine
- 1 cup honey
- ½ cup whole grain or dijon mustard
- 3 tablespoons freshly squeezed lemon juice
- 4 garlic cloves, minced
- ¼ cup soy sauce
- 1 tablespoon fresh thyme, minced
- 2 tablespoons freshly ground black pepper
- ¼ cup olive oil
- 4 pheasants, skin intact and cut in half along breastbone and backbone

Combine first 4 ingredients in a medium sauce pan over medium heat, bring to boil and stir to blend ingredients. Remove from heat, cool, add garlic, soy sauce, thyme and pepper and whisk in olive oil, a little at a time. Rinse pheasants in cold water and pat dry with paper towels. Place in a container and pour marinade over pheasants. Cover and refrigerate for 12 hours, turning occasionally to marinate evenly. Remove from marinade and allow to air-dry for one hour before smoking. Place in a water smoker or a dry smoker with a pan of water placed close to the heat source. Smoke for 3 to 4 hours over low heat (approximately 150° F) or until pheasant breast reaches internal temperature of 145° F.

SIDE DISHES

A handful of my favorite accompaniments for wild game dishes may be found in this section.

Your choice of side dishes should be dictated by what is available at your local market. I usually visit the produce section *before* choosing a side dish, so that I can determine which seasonal fruits, vegetables and herbs look good at the time. Although much of the produce appearing in our markets is available year around, the flavor of those items which have been imported are usually not as pronounced as ripe local varieties.

Choose side dishes that complement your main course in both color and flavor. If your game dish is dark in color, prepare a colorful side dish such as an assortment of mixed vegetables. Monochromatic plates are less pleasing to the eye than those that have been assembled with more thought and planning. If my choice of entrée is based on a selected ethnicity such as Thai or Asian, I select side dishes that are indigenous to the region, but do not contain the same ingredients as the entrée. Thusly, you won't bring together two similar dishes that compete with each other.

BOAR FRIED RICE

4 servings

- ¾ pound wild boar trim, fat removed and diced into ¼ inch cubes
- 2 tablespoons peanut oil
- ½ teaspoon salt
- ½ teaspoon sugar
- 1 garlic clove, minced
- ⅓ cup green onion, diced
- ½ cup celery, diced
- 2 cups chilled cooked white rice
- 1 cup bean sprouts
- ¼ cup soy sauce
- 3 eggs, lightly beaten

In a wok or large skillet over high heat, heat oil and add boar, salt and sugar. Cook for 3 - 4 minutes. Add onions, celery and garlic and stir-fry for 2 minutes. Add rice and bean sprouts and stir-fry for 1 minute. Stir in soy sauce, move rice to sides of wok or skillet and add eggs to center. Cook eggs until set, scramble and stir into rice.

CORN CAKES

4 servings

- 2 cups fresh sweet corn kernels
- ⅓ cup red bell pepper, diced fine
- ¼ cup green onion, diced
- ¼ cup fresh cilantro leaves, minced
- ½ cup seasoned bread crumbs
- 1 teaspoon baking powder
- ¼ teaspoon salt
- ⅛ teaspoon freshly ground black pepper
- 2 eggs
- ¼ cup peanut or vegetable oil

Combine all ingredients except oil. Mix thoroughly. Divide mixture into 4 equal portions. Divide each portion in half and form a small patty out of each piece, pressing down between your hands to firm up each cake. Heat oil in a large skillet over medium-high heat. Brown each cake lightly on both sides. Serve immediately or transfer to a baking dish, cover with foil and keep warm in a 200° F oven for up to 30 minutes.

WILD RICE PILAF

6 - 8 servings

- 4 ounces butter
- 1 medium onion, chopped
- 2 celery stalks, diced
- 1 large carrot, diced
- ½ cup slivered almonds
- 1 cup wild rice
- 1 cup brown rice
- 2 cups fresh mushrooms, chopped
- 2 cups game stock, game bird stock or beef broth

In a large skillet, melt butter over medium-high heat and sauté next 4 ingredients for 2 to 3 minutes. Add rice and mushrooms and sauté for 4 minutes more. Transfer contents of skillet to a casserole dish, stir in broth, cover and bake in a pre-heated 350° F oven for 1 hour.

GARLIC MASHED POTATOES

4 -6 Servings

- 3 pounds baking potatoes, peeled and quartered
- ⅓ cup sour cream
- 2 tablespoons butter
- 3 garlic cloves, roasted in a 350° F oven until softened and lightly browned, then mashed into a coarse paste

salt and pepper to taste

Place potatoes in a stock pot, cover with water and add 1 teaspoon salt. Boil, covered, for 20 minutes until potatoes are cooked. Remove stock pot from heat. Drain potatoes in a colander, return to stock and mash. Add remaining ingredients and mash until light and fluffy.

GRILLED VEGETABLES
WITH COMPOUND BUTTER

4 servings

6 ounces butter, softened
¼ cup fresh basil, minced
2 tablespoons lemon rind, yellow part only, minced
2 zucchini, sliced lengthwise into 4 slices
1 small red onion, sliced into 4 slices lengthwise into 2 slices
1 red bell pepper, seeded and quartered
2 tablespoons red wine vinegar
2 garlic cloves, minced
½ teaspoon dried basil flakes
½ teaspoon dried oregano flakes
¼ teaspoon chili flakes
¼ cup olive oil

Divide butter in half. Blend one half with basil and the other half with lemon rind. On a piece of wax paper, spread basil mixture on the center to form a rectangle about 1 ½ inches wide by 3 inches long. Place in refrigerator for 10 minutes. Spread lemon mixture over cooled layer. Fold wax paper over, twist ends and form into a cylinder. Place in freezer for 1 hour. Remove from freezer 10 minutes before slicing.

Prepare vegetables as indicated. In a medium bowl, combine vinegar, garlic and dried seasonings. Whisk in oil, a little at a time. Add vegetables, toss and marinate for 1 hour, tossing occasionally. When barbecue coals are ash-white or gas grill is medium-hot, place carrot and onion pieces on grill. Cook until grill marks appear on down side. With tongs, turn carrot and onion over and arrange remaining vegetables on grill. Remove all vegetables when marked on both sides. Cooked vegetables should be a little crisp. Transfer to a serving dish and top with sliced compound butter.

MUSHROOM SAUTE

4 - 6 servings

2 tablespoons butter
¼ cup dry white wine
1 garlic clove, minced
1 pound fresh assorted mushrooms (porcini, crimini, portabella, etc.), hard part of stems removed and caps and stems sliced thinly
salt and freshly ground black pepper to taste
⅓ cup pecan pieces, lightly toasted in a 350° F oven
2 tablespoons fresh parsley, chopped
1 teaspoon fresh rosemary, minced

In a large skillet over medium heat, melt butter, add wine and garlic and cook for 3 minutes. Add mushrooms, cook 4 to 5 minutes, stirring occasionally. Season with salt and pepper. Add remaining ingredients, stir and cook for 2 minutes more.

TWO-COLOR POLENTA

Colorful side dish is a wonderful substitute for standard starch dishes such as rice or potatoes. Great with marinara or grilled red bell pepper sauces.

6 - 8 servings

3 ½ cups chicken broth
½ teaspoon salt
1 cup dry polenta
2 tablespoons butter
1 cup fresh basil, minced
½ cup pine nuts, roasted in 325° F
    oven until lightly browned
½ cup Parmesan cheese.
1 cup gorgonzola cheese, crumbled

In a medium sauce pan, bring chicken broth and salt to a boil. Gradually stir in polenta, reduce heat to simmer and cook, stirring constantly, for 20 to 25 minutes. Blend in butter.

In a blender or processor, add basil, pine nuts and parmesan cheese. Process to mix ingredients and grind nuts. Lightly grease a 9" pie pan. In a bowl, add 1/2 of polenta and mix well with basil mixture. Place contents of bowl into bottom of pie pan and spread smooth with spatula. Rinse bowl and place remaining polenta in bowl. Mix in cheese and carefully spread mixture over first layer. Place in 350° F oven for 45 minutes. Remove from oven and let stand for 1 hour to set. Slice into wedges and warm in a 250° F oven to serving temperature.

POTATO AND APPLE PANCAKES

6 servings

1 ½ pounds baking potatoes,
    washed and peeled
2 Granny Smith apples,
    peeled and cored
2 large eggs
1 medium onion
1 dash nutmeg
¾ teaspoon salt
¼ teaspoon freshly ground
    black pepper
3 tablespoons flour
½ cup vegetable oil

Grate potatoes and apples with a hand grater or food processor fitted with a grating disk. Place grated potatoes and apples into a large bowl of ice water. Let stand for 20 minutes. Drain well and pat dry with paper towels or a clean dish towel. Wipe out bowl and combine remaining ingredients except oil, mixing well. Add potatoes and apples and mix thoroughly to coat evenly. Divide mixture in half and make 6 equal portions out of each. Form each portion into a ball. Add enough oil to just cover the bottom of a large skillet evenly. Heat to medium-high. Place a few portions at a time into the oil, flatten out with a spatula and brown on both sides. Remove cooked pancakes and place on paper towels to drain. Allow 2 pancakes per person.

VEGETABLE WON TONS
Your guests will beg for more.

25 Won Tons

- 1 tablespoon soy sauce
- 2 tablespoons dry sherry
- ½ cup carrots, grated
- ½ cup celery, diced fine
- 2 teaspoons peanut oil
- 2 garlic cloves, minced
- 1 tablespoon fresh ginger, grated
- 2 green onions, chopped fine
- 2 egg yolks
- ½ cup mushrooms, minced
- ⅓ cup water chestnuts, chopped
- 25 won ton wrappers
  - peanut oil for trying

Dipping Sauce:

- ¼ cup soy sauce
- ¼ cup rice vinegar
- 2 tablespoons hot chili oil

In a non-reactive bowl, combine first four ingredients. Let stand for 15 minutes. In a hot wok or large skillet over high heat, heat 2 teaspoons peanut oil and carrot, celery, marinade and next 6 ingredients. Stir-fry for 4 minutes. Remove contents and cool.

Place about 1 tablespoon of mixture on the center of each won ton wrapper. Lightly moisten the edges of each wrapper and fold over, forming a half circle. Press down firmly along all edges. Heat peanut oil over medium-high heat in a small deep sauce pan or deep fryer. Fry won tons a few at a time, until golden brown. Transfer to paper towels to drain. Combine dipping sauce ingredients and serve with won tons.

JULY 4TH GREEN BEANS
Chilled colorful side dish for a warm summer lunch or dinner.

4-5 servings

- ¼ cup chopped fresh basil
- 2 garlic cloves, minced
- 1 tablespoon lemon juice
- 1 tablespoon dijon mustard
- 1 tablespoon honey
- ¼ teaspoon freshly ground black pepper
- 1 pinch salt
- ½ cup rice vinegar
- ¼ cup of olive oil
- 3 cups blanched fresh green beans
- ½ each. red, yellow and orange bell peppers, seeded and sliced into 1/4 inch thick strips.
- ⅓ cup slivered almonds, lightly coated with sugar and baked in a 325° F oven until golden brown
- ⅓ cup crumbled gorgonzola or bleu cheese

In a medium bowl, combine first 6 ingredients. Add olive oil while whisking vigorously. Add remaining ingredients, toss to coat well. Cover and refrigerate for 1 hour.

GAME SAUCES

A flavorful sauce is almost as important as proper game preparation. Unfortunately a common practice among game cooks is to match wild game with a can of prepared soup or a dry soup mix and stew for several hours until the meat is moist and tender. While one cannot argue that the dish is indeed edible, it hardly does justice to that animal which we worked so hard for and dreamed about during the off-season. Pairing a magnificent pheasant with a can of cream of chicken soup and a slow-cooker should, at minimum, be a misdemeanor punishable by disposal of the can of soup at the target range.

I suppose that many people choose the soup/sauce route to take the "gamy" out of game. By following the aforementioned handling and cooking techniques, virtually all offensive flavors are eliminated. Combine a deftly handled game animal with a rich and flavorful sauce and you may even convince staunch non-game diners that they have been missing out on some extraordinary meals.

Several recipes specify utilizing certain parts of an animal, most notably, the breasts of game birds and waterfowl. Small game carcasses are also seldom used in preparation. The best way to make use of the carcasses, bones, trim, legs and thighs is to wrap, label and freeze them until there is sufficient inventory to make a large quantity of game stock. The advantage of homemade stock is a more pronounced and less salty flavor than commercially prepared broths and bouillon. Once a rich stock has been prepared, pour the stock through a strainer, cool and skim off and discard any fat that forms on the top. Stocks can then be placed in small units and frozen. I prefer to freeze my stocks in ice cube trays. Once frozen, I package the cubes in Food Saver VacLoc bags and thaw them out when needed. The Food Saver is also great for storing the above items and preventing freezer burn until you have enough to make your stock.

I prefer not to "drown" game dishes in sauce. If you find that a particular sauce is especially pleasing or popular, offer additional sauce in a serving bowl. When serving, place a small quantity of sauce on the plate, arrange the game artistically over the sauce and drizzle a little sauce over the meat. Garnish with a sprig of fresh herbs or a celery leaf and you are on your way to a well-earned reputation for remarkable game cooking.

GAME BIRD STOCK

Homemade game bird stock offers more intense, rich flavors than canned broth. Don't be afraid to add your own personal touches such as the addition of fresh herbs and seasonings. Freeze usable bird parts until you have enough for stock preparation.

Approximately 1 quart

2 ½ pounds upland game bird carcasses, wings
        and thighs
        all-vegetable pan coating spray
1 large onion, not peeled and quartered
2 medium carrots, not peeled and sliced into 1 inch pieces
2 celery stalks, cut in half
4 garlic cloves, cut in half
2 quarts cold water
3 black peppercorns (or 1/4 teaspoon coarse grind black pepper)
2 sprigs of fresh thyme
2 4 inch sprigs of fresh rosemary
1 bay leaf

Pre-heat oven to 350° F. Spray bottom of roasting pan with pan coating. Place bird parts, onions, carrots, celery and garlic in pan, and spray again to coat lightly. Roast in oven until bones and meat are browned, but not burnt. Transfer contents, including drippings and scraps to large stock pot. Add remaining ingredients and bring to boil. Reduce heat to low and simmer for 6 to 8 hours. If necessary, add water to just cover bones during cooking. Strain, cool and refrigerate or freeze until needed.

GAME STOCK

Make good use of frequently discarded bones to create a marvelous game stock.

Approximately 1 quart

1 ½ to 2 pounds big game neck, back
            and/or rib bones and bird carcasses
2 tablespoons vegetable oil
1 medium onion, quartered, not peeled
1 large carrot, sliced into 1 inch pieces, not peeled
2 celery stalks, cut in half
2 quarts cold water
1 bay leaf
½ teaspoon coarse ground black pepper

Pre-heat oven to 350° F. Rub oil over bones and/or carcasses and place in roasting pan with vegetables. Place pan in oven and roast until bones and vegetables are browned, but not burnt. Transfer contents, including drippings, to a large stock pot over medium-high heat and add remaining ingredients. Bring to boil, reduce heat to simmer and cook, uncovered, for 6 to 8 hours. During cooking, keep enough liquid in pot to cover bones. Add additional water, if necessary. Strain, cool and refrigerate or freeze until needed.

CHERRY CHUTNEY

Game Birds, Waterfowl, Big Game

Approximately 4 cups

2 ½   pounds pitted cherries, fresh or frozen
1   cup diced yellow onion
2   tablespoons fresh ginger
2   garlic cloves, minced
1 ½   cups sugar
2   teaspoons mustard seeds
⅛   teaspoon ground cinnamon
¼   teaspoon celery seed
¼   teaspoon dried red pepper flakes
2   teaspoons salt
⅛   teaspoon ground allspice
½   teaspoon ground coriander
1 ½   cups white wine vinegar
¼   cup light corn syrup

Place all of the ingredients except vinegar and corn syrup into a heavy saucepan. Bring mixture to a boil. Cook until reduced to a thick consistency, stirring often.

Mix together vinegar and corn syrup and add to chutney. Boil down to a syrupy consistency. Remove from heat and cool. Chutney will slightly thicken as it cools.

BROWN SAUCE

A rich, full-flavored sauce which can either stand alone as a game sauce for venison and waterfowl or be used as a base for a multitude of game sauces.

Approximately 1 quart

1 ½ - 2   pounds big game neck, back and/or rib bones
2   tablespoons vegetable oil 1 medium onion, not peeled and cut into quarters
2   celery stalks, cut in half
1   large carrot, cut into 3 pieces
2   quarts beef broth
⅓   cup flour
⅓   cup vegetable oil
2   garlic cloves, sliced
1   teaspoon coarse grind black pepper
1   bay leaf
½   cup tomato purée
½   cup fresh tomatoes, diced

Coat bones with oil and place in a roasting pan with onion, carrots and celery. Place in a 350° F oven and roast until well browned, but not burned. Transfer contents, including drippings, to a large stock pot over medium-high heat and add beef broth. In a small skillet, heat oil until very hot. Carefully add flour, whisking constantly, until *roux* mixture is browned, but not burnt. If roux burns, discard and repeat process. Add finished roux to stock pot and stir to mix. Add remaining ingredients, bring to boil, reduce heat to low and simmer, uncovered for 3 to 4 hours. Strain and refrigerate or freeze until needed.

BALSAMIC
CHERRY SAUCE
All Game Meats

Approximately 1 cup

2 tablespoons Balsamic vinegar
1 ½ cups dry red wine
2 tablespoons brown sugar
2 teaspoons fresh rosemary, minced
1 cup dried cherries
1 tablespoon cornstarch mixed with 1 tablespoon cold water
salt and pepper to taste

In a medium sauce pan over high heat, add vinegar, wine, sugar, rosemary and 1/2 of the dried cherries. Reduce liquid by one half, transfer mixture to a blender or food processor and process for 15 seconds. Return sauce to pan, add remaining dried cherries, lower heat and simmer for 3 to 4 minutes. Add cornstarch mixture, stirring in a little at a time until sauce thickens. Season with salt and pepper.

RASPBERRY
SAUCE
Waterfowl, Upland Game, Antlered Big Game

Approximately 1 cup

1 cup dry red wine
1 cup game stock or beef broth
1 shallot, diced
3 fresh rosemary sprigs
½ cup frozen raspberries, sweetened
¼ cup raspberry preserves
1 tablespoon cornstarch mixed with 1 tablespoon cold water
salt & ground black pepper to taste

In a medium sauce pan over medium-high heat, bring first 4 ingredients to a boil. Reduce heat to medium and cook until liquid is reduced to about 1 cup. Stir in raspberries and preserves and simmer for 12 to 15 minutes. Pour through strainer and return to pan. When there is approximately 1 cup of sauce, increase heat to medium- high. Add cornstarch mixture, a little at a time while stirring, until sauce thickens. Season with salt and pepper.

BÉCHAMEL
SAUCE
A basic sauce frequently used as a base or thickener for a variety of sauces. Create your own sauces by adding assorted ingredients such as cheeses, herbs and citrus juices.

Approximately 1 cup

2 tablespoons butter
2 tablespoons flour
1 cup milk
salt and white pepper to taste

In a medium saucepan over medium heat, melt butter. Add flour while whisking until mixture is bubbly. Cook for 2 minutes, whisking frequently. Do not allow mixture to brown. Reduce heat, if necessary. Gradually blend in milk in a thin stream while whisking and cook until sauce boils and is smooth and thick. Season with salt and pepper.

GRILLED RED BELL PEPPER SAUCE

For use with Upland Game

Approximately 1 cup

1 large or 2 small red bell pepper
½ red onion, sliced into 2 rings
1 tomato, cut in half
2 tablespoons olive oil
¼ garlic cloves, minced
⅓ teaspoon dried red pepper flakes
1 tablespoon red wine vinegar
⅓ cup heavy cream
2 tablespoons fresh basil, minced
    (or 1/2 teaspoon dried basil flakes)
salt and freshly ground black pepper

Brush onion, garlic and tomato with 1 tablespoon olive oil. On a greased barbecue grill over white-hot coals, place bell pepper over hottest part of grill. Place onion and tomato on grill and cook until grill marks appear on both sides. Remove and set aside. Place garlic on foil or small pan and cook until lightly browned. Cook bell pepper until blackened on all sides. Remove bell pepper from grill and place in a small paper bag. Close top of bag and allow to steam for 10 minutes. Remove bell pepper, pull out stem, tear along one side to open up pepper. Remove seeds. Place blackened side out on a flat surface and scrape skin off with the edge of a knife. A few bits of skin won't hurt the finished sauce.

Place all ingredients except cream, basil, salt and pepper in a blender or food processor and purée until smooth. Transfer to a small sauce pan and heat to a boil. Add cream and basil and cook over medium heat for 4 to 5 minutes. Season with salt and pepper.

Note: For a lighter version of the sauce, substitute game bird stock, game stock or chicken broth for cream.

PISTACHIO PESTO
CREAM SAUCE

For use with Game Birds

Approximately 2 cups

1 cup unsalted California
    pistachios, shelled and
    roasted in oven until
    lightly browned
½ cup Parmesan cheese,
    grated
6 garlic cloves, roasted until
    golden brown, but not
    burned
1 cup fresh basil, chopped
¼ cup olive oil
1 cup heavy cream
    salt and white pepper to
    taste

In a blender or food processor, blend 1/2 cup of pistachios, cheese, garlic, basil and olive oil. Transfer to medium sauce pan over medium-high heat and add cream and remaining pistachios. Reduce liquid by one-half and season with salt and pepper.

SWEET AND SOUR
ZINFANDEL SAUCE

Waterfowl, Doves and Big Game

Approximately 2 cups

- 2 tablespoons olive or peanut oil
- 4 garlic cloves, minced
- ⅓ cup yellow onion, diced fine
- ¼ cup brown sugar
- 2 cups zinfandel
- 2 tablespoons Balsamic vinegar
- 1 cup game stock or beef broth
- 1 tablespoon Worcestershire sauce
- 3 tablespoons tomato paste
- 4 ounces butter, cut into 5 pieces
  salt and pepper to taste

In a medium sauce pan over medium-high heat, sauté garlic and onion for 2 to 3 minutes. Add brown sugar and cook until the sugar liquefies and caramelizes the onion and garlic. Add the remaining ingredients except butter, salt and pepper. Reduce contents by boiling, uncovered, until there is approximately 1 1/2 cups of liquid. Remove pan from heat and whisk in butter pieces, one at a time, until sauce is thickened. Season sparingly with salt and pepper. If you need to heat the sauce at a later time, do so over low heat. Do not boil or sauce will separate.

SWEET-HOT
BARBECUE SAUCE

All game meats

Approximately 3 1/2 cups

- 1 tablespoon butter
- 1 medium onion, diced fine
- 2 garlic cloves, minced
- 2 tablespoons lemon peel, diced fine
- 1 cup packed brown sugar
- ½ teaspoon chili flakes
- ½ teaspoon cayenne pepper
- ½ teaspoon salt
- ¼ teaspoon freshly ground pepper
- ¼ cup tomato paste
- 2 8 ounce cans tomato sauce
- ½ cup cider vinegar
- 2 tablespoons Worcestershire sauce

In a medium sauce pan over medium heat, heat butter and sauté onions, garlic and lemon peel until onions become translucent, but not brown. Add sugar and cook for 3 more minutes, stirring often. Add remaining ingredients, bring to boil, reduce heat to low and cook for 30 minutes.

SAGE-PEPPERCORN
SAUCE

Waterfowl, Doves, Antlered Game

Approximately 2 cups

- 1 tablespoon olive oil
- ¼ cup shallots, minced
- 2 garlic cloves, sliced thinly
- ½ teaspoon freshly ground black pepper
- 2 ½ cups game stock or beef broth
- ¼ cup brandy
- 2 bay leaves
- 2 tablespoons tomato paste
- 3 tablespoons butter
- ½ cup zucchini, diced into 1/4 inch cubes
- ½ cup carrot, diced into 1/4 inch cubes
- 1 tablespoon brined green peppercorns
- 2 tablespoons fresh sage, minced
- 1 tablespoon flour, sifted
  salt to taste

In a medium skillet over medium-high flame, heat oil and sauté shallots, garlic and black pepper for 2 to 3 minutes. Transfer contents to a medium sauce pan over medium-high heat and add game stock, brandy, bay leaves and tomato paste. Reduce liquid to about 1 1/2 cups. Add butter to skillet over medium heat and sauté zucchini, carrot, peppercorns and sage for 3 minutes. Sift flour over skillet, stirring in with vegetables. Cook for 2 minutes more. Transfer contents of skillet to sauce pan. Stir to blend, bring to boil, season with salt and remove from heat.

PORT WINE SAUCE

Big Game, Waterfowl, Doves

Approximately 1 cup

   3 cups port wine
   2 shallots, minced
   3 3 inch fresh rosemary pieces
   1 tablespoon sugar
   ½ cup heavy cream
     salt and pepper

In a medium sauce pan over high heat, bring first 3 ingredients to boil. Reduce heat to medium and cook, uncovered, until liquid is reduced to 1 cup. Strain out shallots and rosemary. Add sugar and cream, cook until liquid is reduced again to 1 cup. Season, as desired, with salt and pepper.

LEMON CREAM SAUCE

Duck Ravioli, Game Birds

Approximately 1 cup

   2 cups dry white wine
   1 shallot, diced fine
   2 garlic cloves, minced
  1 ½ cups heavy cream
   ¼ cup fresh lemon juice
   2 tablespoons sugar
     salt and white pepper to taste

In a medium sauce pan over high heat, add first 3 ingredients. Reduce liquid to 1/2 cup. Strain out shallots and garlic. Add cream, lemon juice and sugar and reduce to 1 cup liquid. Season with salt and white pepper.

MUSTARD DIPPING SAUCE

An extremely simple and low-fat sauce for all game.

Apprximately 2 cups

   1 cup whole grain mustard
   1 cup red currant preserves
   2 tablespoons freshly squeezed
     lemon juice
   2 tablespoons fresh basil, minced

In a bowl, mix all ingredients. Use as a baste or dipping sauce for game dishes. You can substitute your favorite preserves for red currant preserves.

PICO DE GALLO SALSA

Salads, Upland Game, Boar

Approximately 2 cups

   2 cups fresh tomato, coarsely
     chopped
   ¼ cup red onion, diced
   1 garlic clove, minced
   2 tablespoons fresh lime juice
   1 teaspoon red wine vinegar
   1 tablespoon jalapeño pepper,
     seeded and diced fine
   ¼ cup fresh cilantro, chopped fine
   1 teaspoon sugar
   ¼ teaspoon ground cumin
   ¼ teaspoon chili powder

Combine above ingredients and refrigerate for at least 30 minutes. Can be stored in a covered container in the refrigerator for up to 5 days.

PLUM SAUCE

Doves, Waterfowl, Game Birds

Approximately 2 cups

  1 ½ cups plum preserves
   ¾ cup applesauce
   ½ teaspoon ground ginger
   2 garlic cloves
   1 teaspoon chili flakes
   1 tablespoon cornstarch
   1 tablespoon soy sauce
   2 tablespoons cider vinegar

In a sauce pan over medium heat, cook plum preserves and applesauce until boiling. Combine remaining ingredients and reduce heat until sauce thickens.

MANGO SALSA

Game Birds, Wild Pigs

Approximately 2 cups

  1 ½ cups mango, peeled and diced
     into 1/2 inch cubes
   ⅓ cup red bell pepper, diced fine
   2 tablespoons red onion, diced
     fine
   ¼ cup fresh cilantro, chopped
   ¼ teaspoon chili flakes
   ¼ cup green onions, diced
  dash cumin
  dash Tabasco sauce
     juice of 1 lime

Combine above ingredients and refrigerate for 1 hour.

SUNDRIED TOMATO PESTO

Upland Game

Approximately 1 cup

⅓ cup pine nuts, lightly browned in an oven at 350° F.
1 cup basil leaves
2 garlic cloves
⅓ cup sundried tomatoes in oil
⅓ cup olive oil
salt and pepper to taste

Place all ingredients in a food processor and blend to make a coarse paste. Season with salt and pepper. To store, cover paste with a little additional olive oil, cover and refrigerate.

ORANGE-BASIL
HOLLANDAISE SAUCE

Delicious on all sautéed light-fleshed game birds. If desired, substitute orange juice and fresh basil with your own favorite citrus fruits and fresh herbs.

Approximately 1 1/2 - 2 cups

4 egg yolks
1 teaspoon dijon mustard
2 tablespoons freshly squeezed orange juice
8 ounces clarified butter
2 tablespoons fresh basil, diced
salt and white pepper to taste

In a double boiler over simmering water, whisk together the first three ingredients. Add butter in a very thin steady stream, whisking constantly until sauce thickens. Season with salt and pepper. Serve immediately.

If you wish to hold sauce and warm at a later time, place in a covered container and refrigerate. To warm, place over double boiler with barely simmering water and whisk constantly until just warm. If sauce gets too hot, it will separate.

CAMP CHEF ™

"I mention Camp Chef stoves in this book. These stoves are terrific for cooking outdoors in campsites, at group gatherings, even in your own backyard. You can learn more about Camp Chef stoves by calling 1-800 650 2453."

-Scott Leysath

"I use my Camp Chef Stove regularly in my catering service and in my own yard. You can easily cook an entire meal for just yourself, or for a gathering of 200 and more guests."

"Camp Chef permits me to cook with heat ranging from very low up to 30,000 BTUs. Great for group cooking, like parties, Scout functions or in support of local natural emergencies."

"You can also barbecue, charbroil vegetables, venison burgers, anything you like with Camp Chef's great grill, which sits on top of the BBQ box. You can also use this box as a smoker or oven."

"The griddle fits neatly on the BBQ box. Pancakes cook evenly and quickly. The griddle is easy to clean and store. Best of all, everything you cook on this griddle will come out great!"

"My Camp Chef carry bag makes it easy for me to carry my stove wherever I go. It's also terrific for storing the stove in the house or garage."

91

GAME FISH

As one of the millions of Americans who grew up with a fishing rod in hand, my passion for catching a variety of game fish grew with every outing. As a young boy, I carved bass plugs out of broom handles and fished local farm ponds for monster-sized largemouth bass. As an adult, I am no more or less successful with expensive commercially-made lures. Our summer family vacation included the long drive down Interstate 95 to Daytona Beach, Florida, where my father taught my brothers and me the art of flounder fishing off a crowded pier. Once I received the coveted driver's license, my spring and summer weekends were spent trout fishing in the Blue Ridge Mountains. Since moving west, I have had the opportunity to fish some of the most pristine and productive trout streams in the country.

During my years as an independent restaurateur, my fishing time was limited, but I was able to improve my culinary skills by preparing fresh-caught striped bass, salmon and sturgeon that others brought to the restaurant for me to prepare for them. One of the most important lessons that I learned about preparing fish for others is that the presentation of the dish is almost as important as the taste of the finished dish. Complementary colors and flavors combined with artfully arranged ingredients can make the difference between a great dish and a mediocre one.

I am firmly committed to the catch and release philosophy of fishing. Not only will this insure that future generations will have the opportunity to catch wild game fish, but I really don't have much of a desire to fill my cooler with fish, only to pack them into my freezer and prepare them at a much later time. Freshly caught fish taste infinitely better than those fish that have been frozen. Although I am primarily a fly fisherman and use barbless hooks, occasionally a fish will get hooked in such a manner that survival after release is questionable. Those are the fish I save for the dinner table.

It is important to keep your fish cold before preparation. The sooner it is on ice, the less opportunity it will have to take on unpleasant "fishy" flavors and aromas. Your nose will give you the best indication of the condition of any fish or shellfish. If your fish smells "fishy," it is difficult to mask the smell and taste when cooked. If you must prepare your improperly stored or handled fish, do so by baking or poaching in aromatic liquids. Should you choose to freeze your catch, make certain that it is cleaned, cooled and tightly wrapped. (The FoodSaver vacuum packaging system is also a great way to preserve fish in the freezer. You can vacuum package the whole fish, just fillets or steaks, and store them conveniently in the freezer. Fish can last up to 2 years when vacuum packed in VacLoc bags). When freezing your fish, take a permanent marker and note the type of fish and date caught on the outside of the package. As an alternative to freezing, share your catch with friends and neighbors when the fish is still fresh.

FRIED CATFISH
WITH A SPICY PUMPKIN SEED CRUST AND CILANTRO TARTAR SAUCE

I prefer a couple of small fish to one large one. Flavors are usually delicate and sweet, and they make an attractive presentation when shingled atop one another. If you are unable to locate shelled pumpkin seeds, substitute shelled sunflower seeds or any crushed roasted nuts.

4 servings

8 small catfish, skin and heads removed
1 cup flour, seasoned with 1 teaspoon salt and 1/2 teaspoon freshly ground black pepper
   vegetable oil for frying

Batter

2 large eggs
⅔ cup flour
1 teaspoon salt
⅓ cup cornmeal
1 cup flat beer
2 jalapeño peppers, seeded and finely diced
⅓ cup red bell pepper, finely diced
1 cup shelled pumpkin seeds
1 teaspoon chili flakes

Cilantro Tartar Sauce

1 cup mayonnaise
2 tablespoons capers, drained
2 tablespoons pitted black olives, chopped
¼ cup fresh cilantro, chopped
1 tablespoon freshly squeezed lemon juice
1 teaspoon dijon mustard
   salt and freshly ground black pepper to taste

To prepare batter, beat eggs in a medium bowl. Add flour and salt to blend. Add cornmeal and beer, a little of each at a time while whisking lightly to blend. Batter should be a little lumpy. Let stand at room temperature for 1 hour. Lightly fold in remaining ingredients.

To prepare tartar sauce, mix all ingredients well and season with salt and pepper.

Heat oil to about 375° F in a deep fryer or deep, heavy stock pot. Dust fish with seasoned flour and then place in batter to coat. Fry for 3 to 4 minutes each or until medium-brown.

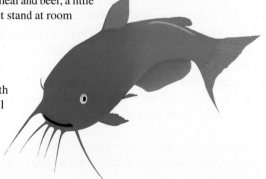

LARGEMOUTH BASS IN A POTATO SHELL

Thin-sliced potatoes, lemon and fresh basil leaves add a protective shell to seal in moisture and flavor.
Serve on a bed of lightly sautéed spinach and red bell peppers for a colorful main dish.

4 servings

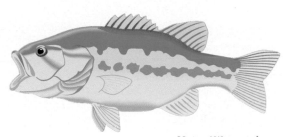

2	cups dry white wine
1	shallot, minced
1	tablespoon lemon juice
4	6 ounce largemouth bass fillets, about 4 inches long, 3 inches wide and 1 inch thick
4	large baking potatoes
1	cup fresh basil leaves
1	lemon, sliced into 8 thin slices
¼	cup vegetable oil
	salt and freshly ground black pepper
4	ounces butter, cut into 4 pieces

Note: When using smaller fillets, you can stack them on top of each other, forming the stacked fillets into the appropriate size.

In a small saucepan over medium-high heat, bring wine and shallots to a boil and reduce liquid to about 1/3 cup. Add lemon juice and set aside.

Wash the potatoes, do not remove skin. Using a sharp vegetable peeler, electric slicer or a very sharp, thin knife, slice the potatoes lengthwise into long paper-thin slices. Slicing the potato as thinly as possible is critical. Thicker slices will break or split when folded. You need to make the potato crust quickly while the just cut slices are still sticky. For each serving lay out potato slices, overlapping edges by 1 inch as you lay them out to form an area approximately 9 inches by 9 inches square. Place the fillet on the center of the potatoes. Season the potatoes and bass with salt and pepper. Place basil leaves and then 2 slices of lemon on top of the fillet. Fold potato slices around fillet and seal top with additional potato slices. Brush top and sides with oil and season with additional salt and pepper. Place in a 425° F oven for 8 to 10 minutes or until potato shell is lightly browned.

Return wine mixture to heat and bring to boil. Remove from heat and whisk in butter pieces, one at a time, until thickened. Season with salt and pepper. Place one portion of bass on each plate and drizzle wine sauce over each.

SMOKED SALMON
WITH GINGER-WASABI SAUCE

Moist salmon fillets are marinated with Asian flavors, seasoned with smoke and served with a enticing sauce.

4 servings

  1 cup low-sodium soy sauce
  ½ cup seasoned rice vinegar
  ½ cup brown sugar
  2 tablespoons sesame oil
  2 tablespoons freshly squeezed lemon juice
  1 teaspoon ground ginger
  ½ teaspoon freshly ground black pepper
  2 garlic cloves, minced
  4 6 to 8 oz salmon fillets, skin intact
  2 cups white wine
  2 tablespoons fresh ginger, peeled and minced
  2 tablespoons prepared wasabi (Japanese horseradish)
  4 ounces butter, cut into 4 pieces
    salt and white pepper to taste

To make marinade, combine first 8 ingredients in a medium saucepan over a medium flame and heat to blend flavors. Let cool. Place salmon fillets in a shallow container and pour marinade over fillets. Cover and refrigerate for 12 hours, turning occasionally. Remove fillets, place on a rack skin side down, and air-dry in a well ventilated location for 2 hours.

In a small saucepan over medium-high heat, bring wine and ginger to a boil. Reduce liquid to about 1/2 cup. Remove from heat and whisk in wasabi and butter pieces, one at a time, until sauce is thickened. Season with salt and pepper. Keep warm over very low heat. Do not allow sauce to get too hot or it will separate or "break." Place fillets, skin side down in a medium-hot smoker and smoke until fish is just-cooked and still moist. Place one fillet on each plate and spoon sauce over each.

POACHED STEELHEAD
WITH PEPPERCORN VINAIGRETTE

I'll never forget the day I witnessed a five-pound steelhead trout caught on fresh salmon roe in a small stream above Chico, California. Unfortunately, the fish was not my catch, but I was fortunate enough to enjoy the fish that night prepared in the following manner.

6 servings

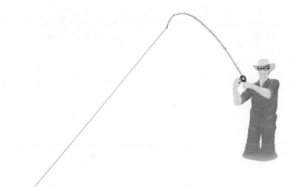

1	quart cold water
2	cups dry white wine
2	cups white wine vinegar
1	large onion, chopped
1	carrot, chopped
2	celery stalks, diced
2	fresh rosemary sprigs
1	tablespoon salt
¼	teaspoon freshly ground black pepper
2 1/2	pounds steelhead fillet(s), skin and head removed

In a large stock pot, combine first 9 ingredients and heat to boil. Reduce heat to low, cover and simmer for 30 minutes. Let cool and strain liquid into a large baking dish, long enough to accommodate the fish. Cover and place in a 450° F oven for approximately 15 minutes or until meat is opaque in the center and bones can be easily removed. Remove dish from oven, remove skin and pull skeleton out carefully. Place equal portion of fish on each plate and top with warmed vinaigrette.

Peppercorn Vinaigrette

⅓	cup white wine vinegar
1	garlic clove, minced
2	teaspoons dijon mustard
1	tablespoon pink peppercorns, crushed
1	tablespoon green peppercorns, crushed
¼	teaspoon freshly ground black pepper
⅓	teaspoon salt
1	tablespoon sugar
1	cup olive oil

In a food processor or blender, process all ingredients except olive oil for 30 seconds. While motor is running, add oil in a very thin stream until emulsified and vinaigrette thickens. Warm in a saucepan over very low heat to serve.

BARBECUED STURGEON
WITH RED PEPPER RELISH

A simple preparation of my favorite game fish that tastes as much like a delicate piece of pork as it does fish. Sturgeon is now raised commercially in many areas. If you are not able to catch one, ask your grocer to order some for you.

4 servings

- 4   4 to 6 oz. sturgeon fillets, cartilage and skin removed
- ¼   cup freshly squeezed lime juice
  salt and freshly ground black pepper
- 1   cup red bell pepper, diced
- ½   cup black olives, chopped
- ¼   cup slivered almonds
- 1   garlic clove, minced
- 2   tablespoons fresh basil, chopped
- 1   tablespoon red wine vinegar
- 2   tablespoons olive oil

Sprinkle lime juice over fillets, season with salt and pepper and let stand at room temperature for 1 hour. Combine remaining ingredients in a small bowl and let stand until ready to serve. Place the sturgeon fillets on a lightly greased grill in a medium-hot barbecue. Cover and cook for 3 to 4 minutes per side or until grill marks appear on both sides. Garnish each with red pepper relish.

BAKED RAINBOW TROUT
IN PARCHMENT PAPER

The parchment paper allows the fish to steam in white wine, butter, lemon and fresh herbs. Serve the fish in the paper, hot out of the oven and watch your guests as they open up the package and take in the unbelievable aroma.

4 servings

- 4   12 to 14 inch rainbow trout, skin and heads removed
- ½   cup dry white wine
- 6   ounces butter, softened
- 1   red onion, sliced into thin rings
- 4   garlic cloves, cut in half
- 1   lemon, sliced into 8 slices
- 2   tablespoons fresh basil, minced
- 2   tablespoons fresh sage, minced
- 2   tablespoons fresh thyme, minced
  salt and pepper to taste
- 4   14 inch circles of parchment paper

In a medium bowl, combine wine and butter, whisking to blend. Place blended butter in refrigerator to firm up mixture. For each serving, lay out one parchment paper circle. Place fish across the center of the paper. Spread 1/4 of the butter-wine mixture over fish. Combine fresh herbs and sprinkle over fish. Set onion rings over fish. Lay 2 garlic clove halves and 2 lemon slices over onion. Season with salt and pepper. Fold paper over, overlapping edges. Fold bottom edge up and over top edge, towards center of the paper. Staple edges securely. Carefully place fish on a shallow baking sheet in a 400° F oven for 10 to 12 minutes. Remove from oven and serve immediately.

FRESH TROUT
WITH CITRUS

A great way to prepare just-caught trout either streamside or in the kitchen. Fillet fish by first placing on a firm surface. Make a knife cut below the head with a sharp fillet knife. Hold onto the head while running the knife blade along the backbone, angling the blade slightly downward, until the side is excised at the tail. Flip the fish over and repeat the process for the other side.

4 servings

- 4-6 fresh trout, cleaned and filleted and lightly seasoned with salt and freshly ground black pepper
- 2 tablespoons olive oil
- 3 garlic cloves, mashed
- ½ cup white wine
- 1 lemon, quartered
- 1 lime, quartered
- 1 orange, quartered
- ½ red onion, cut into rings
- 2 tablespoons butter, chilled

Heat olive oil in a large skillet over medium heat. Add garlic and sauté for 2 to 3 minutes. Place trout, skin side down, in skillet and cook for 3 minutes. Add wine and cook until wine reduces by one-half and meat begins to get firm. Add onion rings. Squeeze citrus fruits into pan and sauté until meat is thoroughly cooked, about 3 minutes more. Remove trout to serving plates. Remove pan from heat and whisk in butter until sauce thickens. Pour sauce over fillets and serve immediately.

MARYLAND
FISH CHOWDER

Growing up in Northern Virginia, I had the opportunity to spend some quality time on Maryland's Eastern Shore feasting on oysters, crabs, scallops and a variety of fresh fish. The following simple chowder recipe can be used with an assortment of freshwater and saltwater game fish.

6 servings

- ¼ cup salt pork, diced
- 1 large yellow onion, diced
- 2 carrots, diced
- 3 celery stalks, diced
- 8 ounces clam juice
- ¼ ounce white wine
  water
- 2 cups potatoes, diced into 1/2 inch cubes and cooked firm
- ¼ cup fresh parsley, minced
- 1 quart whole milk
  salt & freshly ground black pepper to taste

In a medium stock pot over medium-low heat, cook salt pork until lightly browned. Stir in onions, carrots and celery, increase heat to medium and cook for 3 to 4 minutes. Add clam juice, white wine and enough water to barely cover fish. Cover and simmer for 10 minutes. Reduce heat to low, add potatoes, parsley and milk and heat to serving temperature. Stir in salt and pepper to taste.

SALMON GRAVLAX
WITH HERBS AND PEPPER

A real treat when prepared with firm, fresh salmon fillets. the preparation may seem a bit unorthodox if you've never made gravlax-style salmon before, but I am certain that you'll want to try it more than once. Serve as a first course with toast points or crackers with Creole mustard.

8 - 10 Appetizer Servings

- ⅓ cup Kosher salt
- ⅓ cup light brown sugar
- 2 tablespoons each, white, black and pink peppercorns, crushed.
- 1 tablespoon mustard seeds, crushed
- ½ cup fresh dill, chopped
- ½ cup fresh basil, chopped
- ½ cup fresh parsley, chopped
- 1 lemon
- 2 1 pound salmon fillets, skin intact, all bones removed

Combine first 6 ingredients and mix well. Squeeze one-half of each lemon on the flesh side of each fillet. In a long, deep glass or ceramic dish, sprinkle one fourth of the herb mixture on the bottom of the dish. Place one of the fillets, skin side down in dish over herb mixture. Distribute one-half of the herb mixture evenly over the salmon flesh. Place the second fillet skin side down, matching head to head with first fillet. Sprinkle remaining mixture over exposed skin side of second fillet. Cover with a double layer of heavy foil and place two bricks on top of foil. Place in refrigerator for 3 days, turning the salmon 2 to 3 times daily.

Prior to serving. wipe off the herb mixture and pat dry with paper towels. Place the fillets, skin side down, on a cutting board and slice thin slices diagonally across the grain.

GRILLED STRIPED BASS
WITH AVOCADO CREAM SAUCE

Place a piece of lightly greased foil over the barbecue grate and place the fish on the foil to keep It from sticking.

4 servings

- 4 6 to 8 ounce striper fillets, skin removed
- ½ teaspoon ground coriander
- ½ teaspoon paprika
- ½ teaspoon freshly ground black pepper
- ⅔ cup dry white wine
- 2 garlic cloves, minced
- 1 medium, ripe avocado, skin and seed removed
- ½ cup heavy cream
- 2 teaspoons freshly squeezed lemon juice
- 1 dash Tabasco
- *salt and freshly ground black pepper to taste*

Season fillets on both sides with coriander, paprika and pepper. Let stand for 15-20 minutes while barbecue is warming and coals are getting white-hot. When coals are ready, move them to the outside edges of the barbecue. For gas units, set heat at medium. Grill each side of the fillets only until grill marks appear. Total cooking time should not exceed 3 -4 minutes per side.

To prepare sauce, add wine and garlic to a small saucepan, bring to a boil and cook uncovered for 3 to 4 minutes. Transfer to a food processor or blender. Add avocado and process until purèed. Add remaining ingredients, process for 3- seconds to blend, then transfer contents to saucepan, season with salt and pepper and warm before serving. Place one cooked striper fillet on each plate and drizzle sauce over half of each fillet.

WILD GAME MEAT
IS JUST A PHONE CALL AWAY

The following companies specialize in providing retail customers with a wide range of wild and exotic game products. They will ship practically anywhere.

TESIO MEAT COMPANY
1025-1045 East 12 St.
Oakland, CA 94606
800-573-6328 (573-MEAT)
http://www.tesiomeat.com

GAME SALES INTERNATIONAL
P. O. Box 5314
Loveland, CO 80538
(970) 667-4090

CZIMER FOODS, INC.
13136 W. 159th St.
Lockport, IL 60441
(708) 301-7152

D'ARTAGNAN, INC.
399-419 St. Paul Avenue
Jersey City, NJ 07306
800-327-8246

GLOSSARY

Al Dente: Firm to the bite, usually referring to vegetables or pasta.

Baste: To brush with a basting liquid or marinade.

Blanch: To cook for a minute or two in boiling water, stock or fat. Blanching is used to prepare vegetables, fruits and nuts for recipes or to heighten the color of vegetables.

Blend: To mix thoroughly two or more ingredients until smooth.

Braise: To cook with low to moderate heat with a small amount of liquid in a covered pan.

Broth: A liquid derived from simmering meats, bones and/or vegetables in liquid.

Brown: To sear an ingredient with a small amount of fat until browned on all sides. Used to seal in juices and enhance appearance.

Caramelize: To melt brown sugar over low heat until golden brown or to cook vegetables in caramelized sugar until browned.

Cube: To cut into small, approximately 1/2 inch, cubes.

Dash: Less than 1/8 teaspoon.

Deglaze: To add a moderate amount of liquid to a pan to dissolve or loosen cooked food particles, usually done while pan is over heat.

Dice: To cut into very small pieces, about 1/8 to 1/4 inch.

Dredge: To place food in a dry seasoning mixture, usually seasoned flour turning to coat with mixture.

Drizzle: To pour a liquid in a fine stream over food.

Emulsify: To mix usually unmixable liquids. Emulsion is accomplished by adding one liquid to the other, a little at a time, while whisking vigorously or processing in a food processor or blender until liquids become one uniformly consistent liquid.

Julienne: To cut food into matchstick-thin strips.

Knead: To work dough with hands by folding and pressing.

Marinate: To immerse food in a liquid to impart the flavor of the liquid to the food. To rub food with a dry seasoning and let stand for a period of time to enhance the flavor of the food.

Mash: To crush thoroughly into a pulpy paste.

Mince: To cut or chop into very fine pieces.

Pan-fry: To cook over medium or higher heat in a pan in a small amount of fat.

Poach: To cook gently with low heat in liquid, usually seasoned with vegetables, herbs and stocks.

Purée: To make a pulp by mashing, straining or processing food in a blender or food processor.

Reduce: To decrease the volume of a liquid by cooking over medium to high heat, uncovered. The water content of the liquid will evaporate, the liquid will thicken and flavors will be more concentrated and pronounced.

Roux: A cooked mixture of fat and flour used for thickening sauces and soups.

Sauté: To cook quickly in a small amount of butter, margarine, oil or other fats.

Stir-Fry: To cook quickly in a hot wok or skillet seasoned with oil and/or ginger, garlic, soy sauce and other vegetables and seasonings. Cooking is done while stirring constantly to cook evenly.

Whisk: To stir a liquid or batter vigorously with a wire whisk.

INDEX